T0005913

THEORY OF
THE SOLITARY SAILOR

THEORY OF
THE SOLITARY SAILOR

GILLES GRELET

Translated by
AMY IRELAND AND ROBIN MACKAY

URBANOMIC

Published in 2022 by
URBANOMIC MEDIA LTD,
THE OLD LEMONADE FACTORY,
WINDSOR QUARRY,
FALMOUTH TR11 3EX,
UNITED KINGDOM

English language edition © Urbanomic Media Ltd.
All rights reserved.

No part of this book may be reproduced or transmitted in any form or by
any means, electronic or mechanical, including photocopying, recording or
any other information storage or retrieval system, without prior permission in
writing from the publisher.

BRITISH LIBRARY CATALOGUING-IN-PUBLICATION DATA

A full catalogue record of this book is available
from the British Library

ISBN 978-1-913029-96-8

Distributed by The MIT Press, Cambridge, Massachusetts
and London, England

Type by Norm, Zurich
Printed and bound in the UK by
TJ Boooks, Padstow

www.urbanomic.com

CONTENTS

A man who loves to circumscribe himself...
Jean-Jacques Rousseau[1]

NOTICE

This is a book in which the sea enters into theory. A book for a theory which, rather than taking the sea as its object, produces itself as subject *directly on* the sea, occasioned by the world.

Neither a studiously detached case study of a single-handed sailor, nor an essay that takes sailing as its theme as others may take mountain climbing or cycling as theirs, with a view to introducing readers to some philosophy or brand of spirituality, nor a guide in which, donning my sailing instructor's hat, I dispense wisdom about the ocean and the vessels that sail upon it. Nor is it a story of my own travels upon the sea.

Indeed, what would I have to say? I can hardly compare myself to the contemporary offshore racer in their speedboat, the adventurer who sails the seven seas looking to cross new frontiers, or even the traveller for whom sailing is simply a way to visit distant lands.

Racer, adventurer, traveller—the three modes of the solitary sailor. I am none of the above.

But I sail, of course. I have been sailing for almost as long as I can remember—I wasn't even a year old when my parents first began to take me on board with them. As time went on I accrued a variety of nautical experiences, sometimes spending six months of the year sailing, until finally, about a decade ago, I made the decision to spend my life on the water, coming to live on board indefinitely with no plans to return to dry land, fulfilling a lifelong ambition. And I sail alone, most of the time. By inclination and as a rule of method. But never going far—between Ireland and the Azores, let's say. And always choosing windows of opportunity when the weather is right. If I now add that my boat, a robust seaworthy sailboat, eleven metres long, ten tonnes in weight,[2] is manoeuvrable by a single person in all circumstances, it will then be understood that there is decidedly nothing *spectacular* about my maritime activities.

So why have I opted for a title that seems so inherently suggestive of the sea as spectacle?

I understand 'solitary sailor' in a *radical* (or *human, nothing but human*) sense rather than a *spectacular* (or *worldly, all too worldly*) sense. In other words, I seek to wrest this signifier from the regime of worldly labels—including those that designate the sea as a beguiling detour from (yet still of) the world—and make it into a name: *that of humans themselves, of humans shorn of world, restored to themselves.* A name within which, certainly, there resonates something of François Laruelle's 'Ordinary Man' and, even more so, Jean-Jacques Rousseau's 'Solitary Walker', to cite only two of the great trajectories of thought that in some sense pass close to the one I cleave to, the way (I) of a rigorous knowledge of human things (a gnosis, not a human science), (II) of an existential rebellion against the world-thought that is philosophy (a real life, not a realisation). The way—simple, *unilaterally dual, divided, divinised*—of anti-philosophy as rigorous gnosis.

The solitary sailor that I am, without belonging to any of the modes that make up the triplet—high-speed racing, adventurous exploits, far-flung voyages—consequently adds to them another mode, yielding a quadruplet: alongside the sportsperson, the adventurer, and the explorer, the anti-philosopher.

As is usual in such cases, it is the fourth term that is the key to the organisation of the entire fourfold apparatus, which it establishes directly in the real, directly in humans, rather than leaving it adrift in the world: the anti-philosopher, by adding themselves to the triplet of the solitary sailor, subtracts it from the regime of the worldly—the spectacle of which, as utterly crushing as may be, is not all there is. They determine it more radically to attack the worldly, to attack it at its root: the *Sufficient S(p)ecularity (SS)* whose machinations confuse the real with reality and the human with the worldly, laying the foundation for the conformity of humans to the world's realisatory ends, their submission to the endless practical injunctions to realise and self-realise. In short, the anti-philosopher complexifies the figure of the solitary sailor so as to deliver it over to human simplicity, *and so as to oppose to the empire of integral realisation the real rebellion of a way of life with integrity.*

And so, the theory of the solitary sailor is the essaying of an
anti-philosophy.

Not 'an essay in anti-philosophy' as a genre—a genre which, moreover, has scarcely even come into existence,[3] but an attempt to confer a fully positive dimension upon anti-philosophy. To offer something less than a system of anti-philosophy, but more than mere scattered outbursts: an apparatus minimalist yet complete, comprising a *canon* (a *theory of method*) and an *organon* (a *method of theory*), and capable of waging and winning its war of independence against philosophy—of being a 'sovereign heresy' (and not one of those heterodoxies upon which orthodox philosophy preys so willingly that, over the past century, it has taken on the allure of what it has digested, heterodoxy having become its dominant mode of being, its principal manner, as twisted as it is effective, of remaining orthodox). The theory of the solitary sailor does not complicate the figure of the solitary sailor, it complexifies it so as to render it more difficult for the world to grasp, before subtracting it entirely from the world's grip (heretical complexity lies literally at the antipodes of the complications of hetero-orthodoxy, orthodoxy continued by means of heterodoxy, especially 'critical' thought): it radicalises it, and constructs a radical thought from it.

Radical: a thought that grasps things at their root. Which means: the Two of things themselves, in their all-encompassing antagonism. Grasps them and holds fast, refusing both relapse and surpassing, both the yearning for origins and the impulse to progress, the (fusional) One and the (transactional) Three. *The complexity at work here is the coherence of Two, against the false simplicity (the illusory acoherence) of the One and the complications (the incoherencies) of the Multiple.*

The Two, first and above all, of the real and reality: of human and world; of sea and land. And in the last instance, the Two of the real nothing but real and the real of reality, of human and subject, or of human solitude and the solitary sailor. The Two, also, of subject and thought. Of the sailor and sailing. Of (anti-philosophical) thought and (philosophical) world-thought. And the Two of anti-philosophy itself, whose method, an anti-dialectical method, materialising a theory that short-circuits practice, produces as an ethics the heretic who attacks the hegemony of realisation.

And how better to make the case for the Two of anti-philosophy (in which method intervenes twice over, as that which is separated from theory and as that which materialises their discord, yet to come)[4] than by coining, with a condensation that loses nothing, the word 'herethics'? This book could then be understood as the establishment, directly on the sea, of a *herethics*. The essaying of a marine herethics.

*

But not only marine.

The sea, although essential and primordial, is not the only element of this herethics. There is another element, decisive enough to demand, if not a problematisation (which is not the object of this book), at least a thematisation; an element I have only gradually, imperceptibly come to accept over the course of the decade spent writing the few pages that follow,[5] pages which, in turn, have increasingly found their privileged space of writing and their primary outlet within it.

That element is the internet, open, like the sea, to navigation.

This book, then, essays a *herethics of navigation*.

DEDICATION

Too nautical for intellectuals, who know only the land; too theoretical for seafarers, who swear by life alone, this book will hold little appeal for the great majority.

It will not be to the liking of those who, clinging complacently to their individuality as consumers as if to some great treasure, make it a point of honour to read only as spectators, to entertain or inform themselves, to fuel their dreams and reflections, but without ever taking the risk of being subjectively challenged in any way, and who therefore, when they read, do so only from a safe distance, far enough away not to be touched or affected by what they read, and to be able to refuse any consequences in advance.

It will probably receive even less of a warm welcome from those of the spiritualist persuasion, watchdogs of the established order today as they were yesterday,[i] who prescribe that one act as a man of thought and think as a man of action so as to avoid being one or the other, let alone both. They are the most worldly of all, since they combine a hatred of radicality (this constitutes their fundamental worldliness) with membership in fashionable society, and as readers they will be strategically the most virulent, that is to say, tactically the most indifferent, unless some unlikely turn of circumstance forces them to condescend.

Generally speaking, this book will find favour neither among those who are anchored in reality and imbued with pragmatism, and who accept only those parts of theory that lead speculatively back to what they do and how that makes them who they are, nor among their counterparts for whom practice is worthy of consideration only once it has been passed through the sieve of a theory that is valued all the more the fewer consequences it has. The two of them find common ground in their shared hatred of all subjectivation.

---

i. [In reference to *Les Chiens de Garde*, Paul Nizan's polemical 1932 essay against the spiritualism of the leading French philosophers of the era—spiritualism in the sense of a mode of thought characterised by conciliation, pacification, and commerce (P. Nizan, *The Watchdogs: Philosophers of the Established Order*, tr. P. Fittingoff [New York: Monthly Review Press, 1972])—trans.]

Which is not to say that it is for no one.

One always writes for someone; all writing is *addressed*.

It will be objected that, apart from the obligatory acknowledgements and social/professional nods that appear at the beginning of many works, almost all writing is free of any specific address. And certainly, the idiot writes for himself, the scoundrel for as many as possible, the imbecile for everyone in general and no one in particular, and the cretin for posterity.[6]

But ultimately, none of them actually *write*: they ruminate, flatter, communicate, or fantasise. Or, if they do write, if we are to admit that what they do is writing, then I don't write. Which, in fact, may not be such an absurd hypothesis, since they write so easily, out of habit, need, duty, or compulsion, whereas for me putting one word after another to form the slightest of sentences can often be an insurmountable task. While words make their life easy, and they write as easily as they breathe, I don't write—or only just, as if suffocating.

Both nautical and theoretical, this book is in any case made for some, to whom, by virtue of this fact, it is dedicated. Clearly, if perhaps not distinctly, they will already have recognised themselves.

CANON OF CIRCUMSCRIPTION
The Deepest Secret of Humanity
(Anti-Politics)

The place preceding the formula.
Yves Elléouët[7]

ii. [Secularity in the sense of that which relates to the temporal rather than the spiritual—except that the 'secularity' of the world encompasses the spiritual, precisely through the agency of a hegemonic spiritualism—see translator's note i above, and section 14.3 below—trans.]

POINT 0

[0.0] In *The Drummer-Crab*, Pierre Schoendoerffer's great book of honour and the sea, a French Navy dispatch boat comes across a little sailboat, mid-ocean, that has been damaged by a hurricane yet managed to survive the terrible weather by heaving to. 'A solitary sailor', observes the fisheries officer. 'Soon these guys will be the last real sailors...'. This provokes a severe and disdainful reaction on the part of his superior, who replies: 'Sailors, real sailors, are those who make their living, their daily bread, on the ocean'.[8]

[0.1] There are those who go to sea to leave the world behind, to purge themselves of it, and those who annex the sea to the world, who make it as worldly as they can.

A *radical* division—a departure—between sailors as seen by the fisheries officer, a seaman, and as seen by his superior, first and foremost a military man.

This division is such that, in splintering the notion of the sailor, it extracts a point that can be used to break with the world itself, to tear its fabric 'from end to end', as Guy Lardreau says, 'where the eye of the saint can make out a dotted line';[9] it establishes the solitary sailor as gnostic, as *point zero* of an anti-philosophy.

[0.2] The solitary sailor's separation from the world, which follows from their sole existence (existence qua essentially sole redoubled by a deliberately chosen solitude) is as simple and immediate as that which follows from their departure is complex and laborious—unless that which follows is left to its illusory simplicity and allowed to retroactively condition the break from which it proceeds, in doing so engineering its recuperation by the world.

No *specularity* between the simplicity of the break with the world and that which follows from this separation, or else it is *secularity*[ii] that wins out as the world absorbs that which breaks with it. Absorbs it: not just annulling it but feeding on it, using it to eternalise itself the way a question uses its response.[10]

[0.3] Theory of the solitary sailor: at once that which takes the sailor as object and that of which they are the subject, and in this sense not so much theoretical (neutral, indifferent, epistemological) as *theorroristic*[11] (armed, vital, gnostic), it is that which makes it possible to *hold* to the zero point, to endow it with the status and function of an axiom with which to orient a set of theorems whose complexity is a detour—a *method*, literally[iii]—from simplicity.

[0.4] Theorrorism of the solitary sailor: if one draws something from the sea, it is only the voiding [*vide*] of mundanities, their draining out [*vidange*], and the angelic life [*vie d'ange*] which, undoing one by one the knots that hitch humans to the world, one invents for oneself, point by point.

---

iii. [Method, from the Greek μετα-χοδος, *meta-hodos*, the travelling of a path—trans.]

POINT 1

[1.1] *Radical*, that which refuses the world, the society of humans; worldly, that which refuses humans, human solitude.
Radicalisation, the tearing away of humans from the world, is humanisation; *making-worldly*, the moulding of humans to the world, is realisation.

[1.2] Humans hold to the real that they let drop when they come to the world; the world holds to reality foreclosed to the real.
The real is not so much human as the melancholy that condemns humans to radicality; reality is not so much the world as the machine of specular sufficiency whose machinations ensure its secularity.
Melancholy is to humans, and *sufficient s(p)ecularity* is to the world, what divinity is to God.

[1.3] It belongs to worldliness to vampirise humans, to prostitute human solitudes; it belongs to radicality to attack the world, to undo its sufficiency, to deliver to humans their non-worldly lot, their independence.

[1.4] Between the pure figures of worldliness and radicality there runs a gamut of variously proportioned admixtures, two of its principal figures being *worldly radicalisation*, the tearing away of humans from the world via their accommodation to the nothing of world, to the world reduced to the truth of its nullity, and *radical making-worldly*, the moulding of humans to world via a tearing away from this world in the name of some other world.

[1.5] On the ideological plane, making-worldly gives rise to *conservatism*, radical making-worldly to *progressivism* (relativist or absolutist depending on whether it involves a difference of degree or a difference in nature in relation to this world), worldly radicalisation to *nihilism*, radicalisation to *angelism*. A quadripartite set which determines that of philosophy, hypo-philosophy, counter-philosophy, and anti-philosophy.[12]

[1.6] Anti-philosophy supports itself on the real in order to raise up reality, to give it wings: it is an angelism. Making a lever to tear from the world—to save from the world—the tatters of reality, thus suspending point by point the s(p)ecular enterprise, this angelism is a materialism.

[1.7] 'The solitary one', writes Saint-Pol-Roux, is 'a being who, still a human, is not yet a god: it is only a matter of time, a matter of holding fast'.[13] A god, or rather an angel, in becoming: not a 'man of the world' but a human nothing but human, radicalised; a human whose waiting in solitude is an attack on the world.

POINT 2

[2.1] It is first of all a matter of breaking the silence.
Not because speech is preferable to silence,[14] but because only speech has some chance, under certain strict conditions, of saving the essential: precisely, silence. And solitude. The two of which express one another just as speech and the world express one another.

[2.2] For the prattlers whose machinations produce a world in which they can wallow, silence and solitude are inadmissible, because they 'confer upon ordinary things a beauty that goes beyond what can be borne'.[15] Silence and solitude are that in search of which, in search of a *regularity* of which, in my fortieth year,[16] I returned to the boat and to Brittany, a twofold finitude that opens out onto an real infinity, leaving behind me Paris and the imaginary infinity of worldly possibilities.

[2.3] In leaving the intense focus of worldliness that is Paris,[17] it was the world that I was withdrawing from. (To turn one's back on the world in the prime of life may seem rather a grand gesture, but in this case it involved no great renunciation, no career to be sacrificed, for example; the world, it has to be said, had never offered me a warm welcome;[18] without necessarily being a *victim* of anything, I had always felt ill at ease, surplus to requirements, out of place).

[2.4] Withdrawn into some extreme point of myself, at a distance from the world, having taken care of my remaining attachments and those emotional misunderstandings whose half-hearted perpetuation borders on cowardice, possessing only my boat and the stacks of books brought from the shore,[19] far away, and then closer by in Brittany, I had what I wanted: days and days, days uncounted but which added up to years, face to face with the sea.

[2.5] Around me and inside me, the howling of the world fell silent; world-liness had found its antidote.

In this face-to-face with the sea, entirely reduced to the rigorous finitude of my vessel combined with that of Brittany, where the light vibrates and makes everything vibrate, where one can breathe better than anywhere, this land that inspires one to expand into the sea, faced with the setting sun and the great west wind, a far-western land where the grandeur of the West reveals itself—its only grandeur, which yet is immense, that of the infinite extent of its melancholy—here I began to live, parsimonious with my words, flush with things.

[2.6] From being a 'practitioner of the activity of sailing with particular reference to habitable craft', to quote the lofty language of the French Sailing Federation,[20] from being an experienced pleasure sailor but only during holidays, keen to seize any opportunity to enrich my nautical *curriculum vitae* and to rack up—and, of course, be able to show off about—days spent at sea, I now became a sailor *tout court*, a subjectivated sailor.

[2.7] 'I cut myself off from everyone', snaps the oil tanker captain Marco Silvestri (Vincent Lindon) in Claire Denis's film *Bastards* [*Les Salauds*, 2013]; 'That's what the navy is for.'

The sailor, the one whose face-to-face with the sea makes a void of the world. Around them, within them.

[2.8] There are few sailors in the radical sense among *sea users*, as it seems they are called these days.

Whether professional or amateur, most take to the water in order to take something from it, whether for trading, to exploit its resources, to win some sporting trophy, or to test themselves against it all the better to return triumphantly to the world. These are the socialites of the sea.

The dividing line, authoritative, passes between those who make use of the sea, and those who avail themselves of a marine institution.

The socialites of the sea relate the sea to the world to which they them-selves relate; whereas mariners relate themselves to the radical of humanity of which the sea is the mirror.

[2.9] To remain on the water, leaving my vessel for no more than a few hours at a time (only five nights in total over the course of the first five years), encountering very few people, I took up my quarters of the sea, in the sense of 'quarters of nobility'. From that moment on, I have sailed not so as to add something to my life, but because it *is* my life: if not better, at least good.

[2.10] Do you know those transparent days, when nothing is too much, when one is reduced so precisely to the size of one's own finitude that it is the infinite itself that one feels traversed by? Those days when a fine manoeuvre, which is only fine when it blends so well into the landscape that no one notices it, fills the soul without placing the slightest weight upon it? When tracing out a scintillating wake in a warm breeze can make you scream alone into the night?

[2.11] It didn't last. Two years of this mute regime, barely tempered by routine (shopping, administrative obligations and, every now and again, more involved contact with those close to me) and the blessed solitude turned into a banal curse, populating itself with phantasms and phantoms, stirring up rancour and lust. The deeper I made the void, the more gloomy my circumscription became; intensified, the silence lost its vibratory brilliance: far from becoming purer, it mouldered, crumbled, fell to pieces.

[2.12] In the little cell of light which, far from the stereoscopic gaudiness of the world, I had made my home, everything began to resonate hollowly; to reason flabbily.
My face-to-face with the sea became a brainwashing, my soul flushed out and swallowed up.
'Without my realising it', remarks the young lighthouse keeper Jean-Pierre Abraham, 'I had submitted to the stupefaction of aged mariners. Not so very long ago, when I would come down and return to the island after ten days, I would admire them, all lined up on the north quay, immobile, eyes fixed on the horizon. I imagined they were full of wisdom and memories. But now I know that they are empty of all thought. The sea has got in through their eyes, and slowly emptied out the inside of their heads.'[21]

'Ships make you thick', Jacques Brel remarks. 'Your brain rots away because you're always thinking about which direction the wind's coming from'.[22] I'm not sure that a constant concern for wind direction is to blame, but as for the internal atrophy, the apathy of the soul, the subjective desiccation of the mariner, I can vouch for those.

[2.13] Feeding on itself, on its own void rather than on the refusal to take up a place alongside the prattlers who populate the world, the mutism of those who live on the sea, absorbed in the all-devouring, proves inseparable from stupefaction, from brutalisation, from the circularity of weak thoughts, mediocre in their madness, informulable because of their inconsistency, and whose deaf brouhaha, ultimately, in the very end, is no less disastrous than the chatter that makes worldly everything it touches.

[2.14] Start speaking again, then. But not to say just anything. A speech *of* silence: one that comes from silence, and leads to silence. Not to lay down arms and return to the world; but not to take too lightly the fact that I had been undone by my silence. For it is again and always the world which, implicitly, through voiding rather than overfullness, insists, in this naked silence that the sea washes in at the same time as it carries it away.

[2.15] As Maître Folace (Francis Blanche), the notary in Georges Lautner's film *Crooks in Clover* [*Les Tontons flingueurs*, 1963] (dialogue by Michel Audiard) observes: 'Strange, how these sailors have such a way with words.' Strange no doubt in the eyes of the world; far less so, however, if we understand these words as a speaking of silence.

POINT 3

[3.1] Break the silence, then, in order to save it.

[3.2] Speak silence so that silence does not speak, so that it does not make world.

[3.3] Which, contrary to appearances, is not quite the same as saying, with Maurice Blanchot, 'To keep still, *preserving* silence; that is what, all unknowing, we want to do, writing.'[23]
There is idealist silence, which one *intends*, and which retreats as one approaches it, putting thought at its ease as it goes: this is the silence whose dialectic Blanchot enters into.
And then there is materialist, elementary silence, which one *inhabits*, by means of the speech that puts an end to its sufficiency: this is the silence whose anti-dialectic I describe here.

[3.4] The dialectic of silence serves above all as an alibi for the world-traffic of speech, as a justificatory device as sophisticated as it is redoubtably effective, in virtue of which those we might call the *special agents* of worldliness can, with a clear conscience, create, realise and self-realise, while those we might call its *normal agents*, with a clearer conscience (the best in the world, necessarily so) procreate, engender, fabricate flesh for speech.

[3.5] Creation and procreation rely upon one another, together serving to machine, through the fabrication and consumption of the illusions that make us want to live, the infamy of the perpetuation of the world.[24]
And foremost among these illusions, enshrouding them all, is the ideal of silence—silence as ideal.

[3.6] Easy silence, difficult silence. The void of easy silence, the immediate obverse of worldly chatter, is condemned to the swollen rottenness of the margins, which fulfil an essential function for the world: in a notebook, the margin is what holds the pages together. As to the void of difficult silence, it speaks itself. Proffering of the void, harmonic of nothing, the speech of silence recuses both speech and the silence that is its complementary obverse.

[3.7] If speech is orthodoxy itself, easy silence is its heterodoxy, and difficult silence its heresy.

[3.8] To initiate a speaking of silence is to break the heterodox silence in order to establish another, heretical silence, by means of speech. A certain speech the end of which lies outside of itself. A speech that would be a means (a human means, a means of humanisation) rather than an end (a worldly end, making-worldly as an end). A functional speech which operates as anti-idolatry, its functionality being of an iconic order.

[3.9] Iconic: that in the pictorial domain which does not *represent* (representation always stands for itself, has its end in itself) but serves as an avenue of approach, a bridge, a means of access to something other than itself, and which may well be effaced once its task is accomplished. Iconic: that which places into relation what is separated, such as the believer and their God, the icon standing not for a beauty that gives itself to be seen, but for the state—of recollection, of prayer—to which it leads; that which does not furnish the world, does not make a work—or if so then only *as a surplus*, in spite of itself—but, like a stepping stone, supports a tearing away of oneself from the world.

[3.10] Functional speech of an iconic order, the speech of silence protects silence from itself, from its fetishisation which, via a procedure of placing in exception whose dialectic I have described elsewhere,[25] enables the world to make silence one of its keystones. Holding silence in relation to itself, the speech of silence is the dual of silence and of the speech that exists only punctually, undoing the world in a cursive stroke, and not substantially, as discursive regime of making world.

[3.11] To speak silence so that silence does not speak, does not make world, for, as Georges Perros says in a comment on Kierkegaard's *Journal*, 'one must speak a great deal to conceal an authentic mutism'.[26] A great deal, perhaps; but punctually, and only punctually, in any case. The problem being not to conceal one's mutism, but to defend it. It is in this way that the speech of silence, as abundant as there are points to hold to, is on every occasion a minimal speech, in the most compact form possible: a *formula*; formulaic speech.

[3.12] The solitary one breaks the silence only so as to establish it, and to establish themselves within it; that they might remain, and remain in silence.

[3.13] Not to *preserve* silence by writing, but to write flush with silence itself. Formulaic, the speech of solitude is silence held, held back from making world: *theoria* rather than *logos* and the void of *logos*. An anti-dialectic of which, often, the writing of light is more capable than that of words.[27]

POINT 4

[4.1] The sea makes the void of the world without ever making world. It is no more of the world than it is of another world, an alternative to the world: it is the all-devouring.[28]

[4.2] If the sea is not of the world, and is not a world, it is because it is not a reality but the real of reality. It is the living Two, that by and in which creation and destruction, transcendence and immanence, fusion and dispersion, the One and the Multiple reciprocate one another. A reciprocation that is crystallised in the storm, 'at once destruction, overthrow, massacre—and kindness and a sense of harmony and a beauty that is not necessarily tumultuous', in the words of Henri Queffélec.[29]

[4.3] Like the melancholy of which it constitutes the *anti-s(p)ecular mirror*, the sea immerses all reality. Elemental, it determines reality itself in the last instance.

[4.4] The sea, for humans, is opportunity and risk. Voiding the world without replacing it with anything but an abyss, it leaves space open for the world to return, like a kind of miasma, to try and fill the emptiness.. Like air drawn into a vacuum, the world, expelled from the body, comes back in through the window of the soul. Unless it is warded off—which requires, between sea and world, *in place of the void*, a special apparatus: an *institution*.

[4.5] Do not think it is a matter of the sea against the world, quite the opposite: the sea comes before; it is the *ante*-world.
Between the sea, real of reality, and the world, reality, in place of the void, the institution: reality of the real.

[4.6] The institution in its usual, domesticated sense, is an instrument of maximal worldliness: that through and in which the social organisation of humans exceeds its strict adhesive horizontality, and becomes endowed with a depth (historical, genealogical, juridical), with 'roots' which stabilise the self-adhesive social emulsion, providing it with a seating so that the world can hold together.

[4.7] Taken in itself, freed from its domestic straitjacket, the institution is by no means that whose verticality tempers, counterbalances and so, in spite of itself, perennialises horizontal sociality; it is that which attacks this sociality. The institution is anti-social.

[4.8] 'All of this is of no importance, doctor; the second will take my place', as the old sickly commander (Jean Rochefort) declares trenchantly to Pierre (Claude Rich), the ship's medical officer, in the film adaptation of The Drummer-Crab.[30] 'What counts is the ship.' 'The ship?' 'The ship. Men, you know...without a ship, we're not worth much.' The ship is the institution, whose formula the commander enunciates. But Pierre refuses to hear it. For this man who left the Navy long ago only to return later on, at fifty, with a feeling of coming back into the fold ('I had chosen my life...and then, what did it matter? I let go. I was afraid of myself', he tells himself in justification), the institution is a lesser evil, a way traced out in advance for those who lack the strength to follow their own path—or who, like Pierre, have lost their way. For the old commander, on the contrary, it is the institution alone that allows one to hold one's head up in the world.

[4.9] The institution allows humans to stand up straight when the world makes them puddles—or rather, wobbling bowls of jelly.
It subjectivates them, whereas the world socialises them.
The mistake that Pierre makes is to conflate the institution with socialisation, and to consign socialisation to the register of the collective. For individualisation is no less a socialisation than collectivisation is.

What is opposed to socialisation—whether individual, collective, individualist or collectivist—is subjectivation, the human institution.

[4.10] That a human delivered over to themselves, to their own forces, is not worth much, does not mean that the world is worth more than solitude, still less that one must pass by way of the world whether one wants to or not (so that it becomes a question, as repugnant as it is derisory, of the 'acceptable level of compromise'). Which is to say, humans need institutions.

POINT 5

[5.1] The sailor is the solitary one who depends upon the all-devouring inconsistency of the sea to undo the vampiric consistency of the world. Which certainly works, but does not last. Unless one radicalises oneself rigorously, unless one opens one's wings.

[5.2] Method, according to Novalis, is the regularisation of genius;[31] I say the institution is the regularisation of grace.

[5.3] What distinguishes rigorous from worldly radicalisation is their relation to the institution. Both of them articulate a commitment to the void; but the nihilism of worldly radicalisation for which the void is the truth, its method being extinction, sees the institution as a compounding of the lie of life by its sclerosis, whereas the angelism of rigorous radicalisation, whose truth has no being beyond the commitment to the void from which it proceeds, is entirely institutional.

[5.4] The truth of nihilism, an epistemological truth, consummates Enlightenment;[32] the truth of angelism, a gnostic truth, does not so much shed (henological) light as initiate an (anti-ontological) combat against the darkness of the worldly. The angel, alter ego, or partner of the human in this combat is the institution.

[5.5] Terrorism, the corruption of nihilism and of its strategy of the etiolation of worldliness, is the repercussive effect of a fallen radicality and its incomplete making-worldly, its half-digestion by the world. So terrorism is the puke of the world, a world that vomits itself up, and nihilism a worldly anorexia corrupted into bulimia.

[5.6] As reality of the real, the institution places the real into relation with reality by way of the subject, real of reality, to which it gives not hands but wings. The institution is that by grace of which one manages to obtain some *traction* upon realities without succumbing to reality: just enough to live without making oneself worldly.

[5.7] The institution is *anti-prosthetic*, the prosthetic dimension being that which gives hands to humanity, something to fill the void, to make up for its essential ontological default, the fundamental lack of being that makes the human species so poorly adapted for survival. The dimension of the prosthesis or machine evoked by Laurent de Sutter, who observes that 'in all times, the human being has only been able to present itself as such by way of accessories, supplements, prostheses which tell us everything about the human, which is to say that they speak of its absence of being'.[33] Prostheses through the trickery of which humans make world.

[5.8] It is by means of the hands that the human exchanges void (its lack of being) for making (world): real for realisation, melancholy for worldliness.

[5.9] Prostheses: those 'innumerable accessories which', as de Sutter writes, 'from language to fire, from books to computers, from tractors to cosmetics, make us what we are',[34] not placing into relation real and reality but reducing the former to the latter. Plugging the hole of the real with the gag of reality, these prostheses are the way in which humanity completes itself, disencumbers itself of itself.

[5.10] Ennui is the appearance melancholy takes on when humans, disencumbering themselves of themselves, expel it outside, into the exteriority of the world. With their essential void placed at a distance, if not objectivated then at least desubjectivated, they then believe themselves capable of settling accounts via agitation, projects, and all the other worldly acts.

[5.11] If humans accept work so readily, it is in the last instance through fear of ennui, that oceanic sentiment which overcomes those who would rather know nothing of melancholy.

[5.12] Humans have hands because they have no wings, and so as not to have wings; human ontology is prosthetic because it is not institutional, and so as to avoid being institutional. The grip on certain realities that institutions afford to humans is like the ascending air currents a bird climbs to remain in flight. Here, grace is obedience to the law of the air. It is freedom itself, which lies at the antipodes of worldly freedom.

[5.13] Institutional freedom, human rather than worldly, consists not in having choices available, but in organising oneself so as to no longer have such choices. Thus Rousseau, for whom 'the impulsion of mere appetite is slavery, and obedience to the law one has prescribed to oneself is freedom'.[35] And even more so—because it allows less latitude to the world (that play, in the mechanical sense of the term, that is so foundational for the Great Game of worldly individuals, those whose freedom consists in evading themselves so as to make sure to remain captive)—Christian Jambet's theorem, according to which 'freedom is never anything but a subject's act of being when it confronts the absence of world in which the bonds of servitude fall away.'[36]

[5.14] *Freedom is a point of departure, not a horizon.* One only arrives at it if one sets out from it. (Which is not to say that we should not defend *freedoms*, but that is another matter.)

[5.15] 'Free Sein [...] [T]he sea imposes upon Sein its exclusive authority', said Jean Epstein in 1930 after filming *Mor'vran: Sea of Crows* on the Breton island of Sein. 'Why does this tyranny look like freedom from our constrained continental point of view? Why, falling under the hardest and blindest of laws, do I have the impression of frolicking unhindered?'[37]

[5.16] 'So for you, do freedom and imprisonment therefore belong together?' Louis Cozan is asked; to which the former lighthouse keeper replies, 'Well, yes...necessarily so, yes. [...] Freedom isn't doing what you want to do. Freedom is something else entirely.'[38] The lighthouse—an immobile boat, but still a boat in principle. And it is precisely in so far as a boat imposes the maximal constraints that it is the symbol par excellence of freedom.

[5.17] A symbol is not an image, that is to say a representation, and as such homogeneous with the exteriority of the world, but a subjective disposition, a truth into which anyone can incorporate themselves by way of a decision. The confusion between the two, perpetuated by the world, owes to the fact that the symbol *screens* images, which are so many bonds whose network fabricates worldliness.

[5.18] Placing in relation real and reality by acting as a screen between them, the institution does away with the tenebrous s(p)ecularity of their exchange. The (symbolic) screen refuses (imaginary) exchange not by resisting it, but by coming before it: the institutional precedes the prosthetic. The institution is rigorously anti-prosthetic by virtue of being *ante*-prosthetic. Anti-prosthesis of the subject, the institution humanises. *To institute is to give rise to humanity.*

[5.19] In the absence of an instituting of the void of world that the sea delivers, the world will come back, or at least its stale stench will come to haunt the vacant space. To institute the void is to give it a place and, in doing so, to forge its *can(n)on*—in one and the same gesture *norm and explosion*: that which regularises silence and solitude by breaking them. In place of the void, the formula, the place preceding the formula.

POINT 6

[6.1] I say: *Anti-politics, the canonical preceding of the formula by the place.*

[6.2] Politics, the refusal of the priority of the place (*topos*) and its cutting-up by means of speech (*logos*). Politics is that which makes sure that nothing has a place, or has taken place, unless it is inscribed, via speech, into the order of the world (*cosmos*). In which respect politics is always a cosmopolitics—that is to say, a philosophy.

[6.3] Ensuring the absorption of a place by the world is the official function of politics as that which precedes ontology and imposes its law upon it. First politics. It does not move away from the state of things in order to manage it (in the two directions of a management faithful to what is, which opens onto the field of conservative politics, and a transformative management of what is, which opens onto that of emancipatory politics). Rather, it is that which follows from the fact of the plurality of men (Hannah Arendt's definition) or of many speaking bodies (Jean-Claude Milner's rectification), something which despite appearances does not indicate any modesty on its part: political speech—the Word—makes being, assigns to being, assigns to the order of things.

[6.4] The world is not a place, nor even the place of places, but a process: a process of opening in all directions, the world does not *define* itself, properly speaking; indefinite, open, plastic,[39] the world is a making-worldly. To which the human need for closure is opposed. The opposition of the closed and the open, the most profound secret of humanity? Like Frédéric Worms,[40] I believe so—but unlike him, I speak for the closed.

[6.5] Without circumscription humanity is transmuted into 'human resources'. One does not accede to the infinite via the indefinite but via the finite. One does not struggle against withdrawal by opening oneself to the boundless ocean, since withdrawal is the very *condition* of boundlessness. Again, it is important not to wilfully underestimate withdrawal, and the open sea.[41]

[6.6] A place cannot be reduced to a location within the world, and may even escape the world, as that which separates and protects humans from the world. A place is *in* but not *of* the world; it is an in-between. Michel Le Bris: 'It is decidedly to be believed that a "here" is only a place if it is a door...'.[42] The point being: to live in a place is to be kicked out of the door of your home.

[6.7] From the political deactivation of the place there proceeds the cosmopolitical maxim 'I'm at home everywhere'. To which is opposed not the identitarian 'my home is my home' (a foil that cosmopolitanism needs just as the state needs terrorism, even if that means having to secrete it), but the anti-political 'I am at home nowhere'. The at-home is s(p)ecularisation of the place, and politics is its manufacture on all scales, from the microcosm to the macrocosm. The place is the institution of the void; anti-politics provides its canon, the snubbing of the at-home by a solitude endowed with regularity.

[6.8] The world is eternalised by one's chattering at home, even if only to silence oneself; one saves oneself from establishing oneself in the place of the void, and from speaking its word. Without a place, no formula: only chatter, ideally deliberative, which s(p)ecularises places. Whereas for anti-politics, nothing has taken place but the place.

[6.9] Rebellion against the world by way of silence and solitude flush with the sea requires the place and the formula—their canon. The rigorous radicalisation that is anti-philosophy must be anti-politically rooted.

POINT 7

[7.0] The place, as in-between or copresence of here and elsewhere, is gnostic. To say 'I am at home nowhere' is to conjoin exile with the quest for the kingdom and the very failure of this quest. It is to say: I am here, but I am not *of* here. Melancholy—the science of the place. In coming to the world, humans lose themselves in the shadows; there they struggle to rediscover the scraps of light from which they are descended. Such is the logic of the gnosis harboured by the *Matter of Brittany*.[43] And for good reason: places where the land ends are pure places.

[7.1] For a long time I took the place to be accessory or contingent in relation to the formula, which alone was charged with dignity and necessity. Whether one is here or there, I thought, it matters little—or only negatively—since the place is only that from which generality must be abstracted in order to come forth.

A Breton exiled at the age of fourteen, I felt a faint stirring of the soul every time I stayed in Brittany, but I refused to draw any kind of conclusion from this for the purposes of my research,[44] failing to see how a place could not be homogeneous with the body, itself the prison of the soul.

[7.2] But then I began to acknowledge that which *takes place* in the formula. That the soul must become body in order for the body to become soul. The body, prison of the soul? Not exactly. The flesh, prison of the body, first of all.

Distinguishing between body and flesh opens up the possibility of a place that would not be a location—that is to say, a circumscription that would free one from the prison of the world, the rigour of its finitude being precisely what grants access to the infinite.

This circumscription was—and indeed still is—my boat, which for this reason is named *Théorème*: the place of the formula and the formula of the place.

[7.3] A fine discovery, no doubt, this making a void of the world, draining it out. Far less so, however, if one must live in it, trying to invent within this very emptiness a life that would impart some positivity to the rebellion against the world. Because to void the formula of all determination apart from its floating place is to prohibit the formula itself from being anything other than *floating*, and hence from having any grip on the slightest reality. Instituting the finitude of the place as a means for the formula and the formula as determination of the place flush with the infinite, I did not so much find the place and the formula as short-circuit the two terms through one another. What is lacking in the place is the rootedness which, preceding the formula, would give it its constant. And that is what Brittany is.

POINT 8

[8.1] I discovered that I am Breton. That Brittany, gnostic Brittany, is not made for the world, even though the world has annexed it.

[8.2] That for nigh on five hundred years Brittany has been attached to France, and has during that time progressively dissolved into it, owes first of all to the fact that it sees itself as attachable to the world, and soluble in it. No discontinuity between Brittany and this immediate figure of the world that France represents for it: the two are on an equal footing on the political plane. Even before Brittany had lost politically to France, it had already lost simply by being political.

[8.3] Enough Breton mysticism. Not that there isn't an immediate experience of Brittany, but because mysticism is not so much that which degenerates into politics[iv] as the counterpoint politics uses to make us swallow its worldly pill.

[8.4] Neither political nor mystical, Brittany, gnostic, is anti-political. As Alain Le Cloarec writes: 'If, in the nineteenth century, Brittany appeared principally as a means for the affirmation of conservative political ideas, in the twentieth century progressivist and revolutionary ideas would also serve as means for the affirmation of Brittany.'[45] Perhaps in the twenty-first century Brittany will cease to relate itself to the world, whether as the means of one politics or as the end of another; perhaps it will constitute itself once and for all as a *place*, establishing itself in itself, in its finitude which ensnares the infinite, *so that, no longer attaching itself to anything, it will depend only upon itself.*[v]

---

iv. [Charles Péguy: 'Mysticism degenerates into politics'; 'Everything begins in mysticism and ends in politics'—trans.]

v. ['Under pressure from all sides, I remain upright because I cling to nothing and lean only on myself'—Rousseau, *Reveries of the Solitary Walker*, 'Eighth Walk', 126—trans.]

[8.5] There are many reasons why Brittany, understood as the nation of nine lands (Cornouaille, the pays Vannetais, the pays Nantais, the Léon, the Trégor, the pays de Saint-Brieuc, the pays de Saint-Malo, the pays de Dol, the pays Rennais), can and must work toward its independence. Historical, geographical, linguistic, and even economic reasons, in many cases quite valid ones, but the empirical nature of which, since it leaves the radical of Brittany untouched, is as likely to weave its political shroud as to materialise it anti-politically. Determining the empirical set of reasons that militate for independence without being determined by it in turn, the radical of Brittany gives independence the wherewithal to escape the deadlock of unsatisfied demands: its rigour in the last instance.

[8.6] In the same way and for the same reasons that anti-philosophy must be capable of conducting and winning its war of independence against the world-thought that is philosophy or whatever takes its place,[46] so Brittany must be capable of conducting and winning its war of independence against its figure of the world, France. In giving the place its due, anti-philosophy roots itself anti-politically, which, in turn, draws Brittany itself back to its radicality.

[8.7] Brittany calls for something quite different from the fate that has befallen it in the context of its annexation by France. But let there be no mistake about it: Europe is not preferable to France, and cannot provide a new horizon to which a Brittany separated from France could turn. To play Europe off against France, as a number of Breton regionalists and autonomists do, whether out of conviction or pure opportunism, is to complete the dissolution of Brittany into the world, the world reduced to the reign of the globalised market (Europe, or in any case that which today squats on the signifier 'Europe' and which, under cover of a hypocritical pacifism that no longer fools anyone except those who want to be fooled, functions only to break down all resistance to a globalisation whose hegemony *tolerates* only those identitarian particularisms that it *needs* to feed on—until it comes up against its own absence of limits and dies of its own success, once there are no more alterities left to grind up.

[8.8] Among the Bretons fighting for Brittany today, I see only an arc between identitarians and businessmen, passing through various admixtures of the two. The identitarians, however sincere they may be, would collapse in on themselves if they did not have a 'Jacobinism' to oppose (something which, moreover, they would find it hard to give any kind of definition of, preferring to wave the disgraced word around like a voodoo doll). As for the businessmen, identitarians of circumstance and in some cases of pure semblance, they dream of a less French Brittany all the better to dissolve it, via Europe, into the great cauldron of all-out commodification.

[8.9] Brittany is a country, France is not. France—and this is its greatness and its impoverishment—is a *national formalism*. Its greatness, as extreme as it is rare and sequential, has made it a beacon of humanity. Its poverty, abyssally abject when its formalism, instead of being subjectivated, is reduced to viscerally thoughtless bourgeois management and to the armed wing that serves as its centralised administration, devoid of soul and situational intelligence, renders any rebirth of the French phoenix yet more unlikely. In fact, at the point of debasement and concerted desubjectivation at which we have now arrived, any rebirth of France would be a miracle: a resurrection in the strictest sense, the idea of which, regardless of its possibility, no longer holds much interest for me.

[8.10] Brittany is a country, a nation even, the 'nation of nine lands'. But it is not a nation among nations, and cannot become one without bringing catastrophe upon itself. Brittany is a country, but not in the sense in which it would need to champion an identitarian substance against the French state abstraction and take up its place in the dialectical concert that orchestrates cosmopolitical worldliness. And for good reason: *there is no Breton identity in the last instance.* Such an identity only emerges, and for the worse (indeed, one can never be sure that it won't get even worse), when the empirical set of all the various kinds of arguments for the independence of the country, as consistent as it may be, is left to itself, to its spontaneous empirical sufficiency.

[8.11] Brittany is a country, the country of the real, the country which is not of the world and which resists the world. And therefore resists France. This is already the subtle meaning of Cioran's observation: 'There is a French poetry, but there is nothing poetic in French life (apart from Brittany before tourism)'.[47] But it is above all that which flares up beneath the more unlikely plume of Jules Michelet, the preacher of Republican France par excellence, when he sets up Brittany as 'the resistant element of France', discerning in it 'a genius for indomitable resistance and intrepid, stubborn, blind opposition'.[48] Entirely caught up in his grandiose enterprise in the service of the French national formalism, Michelet nonetheless senses, even if he does not want to think it—or not until the very end—that Brittany, which *alone* lends France its resistance, resists France also, resists the world, is not really of the world.

[8.12] An apparent resistance only, not 'blind' but seen from the vantage point of the world or reflected in the world, since rigorously speaking *it is not Brittany that resists the world, it is the world that resists Brittany*, in exactly the same way that anti-philosophy, which, since it precedes philosophy, is *ante*-philosophy, does not resist philosophy so much as philosophy resists it.[49]

[8.13] Brittany is anti-worldly because it is *ante*-worldly, because it comes before the history of the world, because it determines the world from the vantage of a *pre*-history. An antecedence that is not chronological (even if the recent validation, by a large comparative study, of the hypothesis that Armorica was the sole focus of megalithism, lends support to my argument here)[50] but radical, purely transcendental. A precession that finds an exemplary testimony in the words of Jean-Pierre Abraham, arriving one day at the Pointe de Pern on the island of Ouessant: 'No doubt this is the place where storms are the most spectacular, but the waves of foam mask everything. On this occasion, in the slight north wind of the first day, which made for a very choppy sea, scintillating in the bright transparency of the air, I confess: on this spot I was gripped by a true fear. *By a prehistoric emotion.* Here there is no more debate, there is no joking [...]. Pern is a place to die.'[51]

[8.14] 'Here I discovered the truth of the world.' Saint-Pol-Roux had these words inscribed on an entablement of the baroque manor house built for its views, facing the sea on the heights of Camaret, near the megalithic alignments of Lagatjar. A truth the poet approaches when he observes that 'the Earth [or what he also calls 'the entirety of Life'] has never yet existed. Or rather, it may have existed during what is called Prehistory. It ceased to exist during History'—'this pent-up pride of human ants [which] has delayed by a few millennia' what will once more come to exist in the Posthistory he foresees and toward the advent of which he works. Against the historical eternalisation of the world ground out by the machinations of sufficient s(p)ecularity, it is a question of 'putting the serpent's tail in its mouth: posthistory–prehistory. The future is only a past that wants to become eternity once more.'[52] And the Brittany that must be called *canonical*—'Oh Brittany eternal like the Universe!'[53]—is the place of this short-circuit.

[8.15] At which point we discover that the anti-political involves an anti-history. Brittany is anti-political because it is anti-historical. There is the reality of Brittany, which makes history (even if only because, according to all those who want to see it rise, or rise again, on the world stage, history has not given it its due); and there is its real, its anchoring not so much in (empirical) prehistory as in *a* pre-history (transcendental, *here present always to come*) which gives it not only to remain even though it may in fact be eaten up by the world, but also *to be that which remains*.

[8.16] To bring into confrontation Brittany and the world—that is to say, human closure on one hand, worldly flux and opening on the other,[54] *firstly and above all within Brittany itself*. A confrontation such that, in spite of the sufficiency of the reality that stands in its way,[55] seeking to foreclose it, the radical of Brittany insists, and is felt—one can experience it (a 'transcendental experience'—that veritable monster for philosophy, even if various spiritualities, with which anti-philosophy, to understate the case, has no affinity, have overused the expression to the point of trivialising its scandalous nature).

[8.17] Infallible, Brittany separates Brittany from the world.

[8.18] There is no Breton identity. What Brittany allows to be experienced through Brittany, despite Brittany, is humanity itself. Here humans can experience themselves, know their radicality which reality conjures away, learn that they are *in* the world but not *of* it. Gnostic, Brittany is that over which the world, which has annexed it, eaten it up, has no hold. That which defects, always, from the world, and undoes it in order to cut into its sufficiency, being *in* it without being *of* it.

[8.19] Far from Brittany and the world being like part and whole, or, less trivially but just as illusorily, regarding one another suspiciously through a window that prevents them from sharing anything but an indifference that is a mask for hatred, Brittany determines the world in the last instance. Not being of the world and not making world itself, Brittany determines the world without being determined by it in return. No reversion, no symmetry between the two, no s(p)ecularity, just a one-directional and one-sided determination, going from Brittany to the world.

[8.20] Brittany: to not make world while welcoming all worldliness, *to despise hardly anything.* As Perros's theorem has it, 'all the countries of the world are in Brittany, Brittany is nowhere but in itself'.[56]

[9.1] There is no Breton world, there are Breton solitudes. One is not Breton, one can live Brittany and make it live only in, by, and for solitude.

[9.2] The Breton is not really the one who lives in Brittany, or was born there—although it may help—but the one who, withdrawn to the extreme point of themselves, is inhabited by Brittany. 'Hence', writes Anatole Le Braz, 'Breton humanity is to a unique degree in harmony with the Breton soil and is the sovereign completion of its image. A country where nothing dies, a people who pride themselves on having abdicated nothing—such is the singular anachronism presented by Brittany.'[57] An *oriented* in-between of sea and world, of real and reality, Brittany, with no identity to defend or to dissolve, is that which remains.

[9.3] Brittany is that which remains, it is *constant*, in the sense of that which is radical, does not change, escapes the flux of the realisation of the world, and in the sense of the quantity in a formula that remains invariable while others, which it makes possible to bind together, may increase and decrease. For, to cite Perros once more, 'Brittany is only what it is. In it, all solitude is powerfully assisted, relayed, reduced to nothing.'[58]

[9.4] If there is a Breton people, it is a people of solitaries, a negative people, *the people of those who have no people*. As soon as it is taken for a positive people, it negates itself and destroys Brittany, makes it worldly, delivers it over to the world. On the basis of this negative being, what could it possibly mean to work toward the independence of Brittany and for the relief of its people?

[9.5] The independence of Brittany is not to be gained within the world, as a nation among other nations; it is an independence *from* the world. That is to say, Brittany really does not need to 'win' its independence, since as last instance it is always already independence itself, inalienable in the world. It needs only to be, not *recognised as such* by the world, but *known as is* by humans.[59]

[9.6] No doubt it is less a matter of raising up the Breton people than of raising up the world, using Brittany as a support. 'It is the solitaries that guard the equilibrium of the world, because they are at the pivot, at the centres—they glide over the anthills not because they are angels, but because they are winged ants', writes Saint-Pol-Roux.[60] If, as was stated above at the threshold of the Canon, solitaries are separate from the world by virtue of their mere existence,[61] then in order to be more than winged ants, the world's rebels or worldly rebels, they need to support their rebellion upon the rock, the radical, the remainder, in the sense of what remains when the world has passed—in short, the *manance*[vi] of Brittany.

[9.7] In the general formula of human things, which is that of the great rebellion against the world, Brittany occupies the place of a universal constant.

---

vi. [A neologism introduced in the author's *Le théorisme, méthode de salut public* (Montreuil: Éditions Matière, 2006), *manance* denotes that which remains, namely, the tenor of the real nothing but real that is the essence of humans. The term is intended as a radicalised reprise of the Neoplatonic *remaining* (μονή, in French *manence*), the phase of rest prior to procession and return in the emanation of the *Nous*. See 'Proletarian Gnosis', tr. A.P. Smith, *Angelaki* 19:2 (June 2014), 93–98— trans].

ORGANON OF SAILING
To Traverse and Allow Yourself To Be Traversed
(Anti-Erotics)

To know is to traverse.
To love is to allow oneself to be traversed.
Vincent La Soudière[62]

POINT 10

[10.1] The preceding canonical points, which together make up an anti-politics of the solitary sailor, deliver the prolegomenae to Brittany.[63] Now, prolegomenae are given in advance of a science. And this is indeed what is at stake here: to establish Brittany as science, or more exactly as gnosis: not a worldly science but a human knowledge.

[10.2] Brittany is only really *gnostic* in so far as it is not just 'gnostic', but a gnosis.

[10.3] Above I dealt with the canon *of* circumscription in the subjective genitive: circumscription's can(n)on, that is to say, the apparatus of norm and explosion that circumscription requires in order for its rebellion against the world to be more than a mere pretence. Now we turn to the canon *of* circumscription in the objective genitive: the can(n)on that is constituted by circumscription, that is to say the organon of sailing. If circumscription's can(n)on is gnostic, that to which it owes its emergence, namely the organon of sailing, is a gnosis.

[10.4] There is no great opposition between canon and organon, but also no passage from one to the other without discontinuity. Rather, there is a superposition. Because the canon is reprised by the organon to which it is a prelude (in the order of exposition if not that of genesis, canon and organon being concomitant from that point of view). *Both* canon *and* organon, the organon of sailing standing to the canon of circumscription somewhat as reason stands in relation to the understanding,[64] that is, *the canon itself envisaged in its productive dimension*.

[10.5] To take up the canon once more by way of the organon, to reprise it in the twofold sense of *repeating* and *correcting* it via inventive amplification—such is the impetus driving the 'passage' (which is not a passage, or is a passage in place, in a certain sense) from predicate (gnostic) to noun (gnosis)—not so much from object to subject as from the subject to its subjectivation.[65] Subjectivation is the reprise of the subject to which it owes nothing but its occasion.

[10.6] The organon is distinct from the canon only in so far as it is the canon's deployment according to time. Set out in space, the canon establishes the statics of rebellion via circumscription. Set out in time, the organon establishes its dynamics via navigation, sailing, which is circumscription repeated *but with a displacement each time.*

[10.7] Sailing repeats circumscription by displacing it. And Brittany, established as gnosis and not merely elucidated as gnostic, is the organon of sailing.

POINT 11

[11.1] Gnostic is the one who says: *The world? Not for me. I am in the world, but not of it.* And canonical Brittany is gnostic. To invoke gnosis, a word at once scholarly and savage, the name of the division itself divided, allows one to add: *I am only passing through. In fact, I'm leaving. See my wings.*

[11.2] The predicate poses a danger which the noun must stave off. This danger, internal to anti-philosophy, relates to the definition of its angelism, thus far solely materialist—and further, to the definition of a materialism whose imagery of the *lever* flirts with its more rudimentary incarnation, mechanism. Via what looks superficially like a paradox, it is in so far as it is materialist that Brittany is established as gnostic. Now, anti-philosophy is, at once and identically, a materialism and a gnosis, the two terms saving one another from their respective missteps. The anti-philosophical Two applies first of all to anti-philosophy itself.

[11.3] Giving the place its due, anti-philosophy finds in Brittany an anti-political rooting which, in turn, reduces Brittany to itself—that is, not to an identity but to its radicality. And it is by supporting itself upon the radical of Brittany as a kind of Archimedean point that anti-philosophy avails itself of the materialist means for its angelism, since it thereby becomes a lever capable of raising up the world. A modest enough proposal, despite appearances—no ambition to raise up the world so as to turn it upside-down, since the world thrives on such overturnings; just the determinate objective, *here present*, to be able to breathe easy, to be delivered of the weight of the world by virtue of the grace of the institution: to render the rebellion against the world *liveable*.

[11.4] Brittany endows the solitary one, and the floating place of the solitary sailor in particular, with a rootedness which, preceding the formula of rebellion, furnishes them with their constant. This makes Brittany something like the pineal gland of the rebellion of humans against the world: the point at which thought and extension, soul and body, theory and method are joined—and *necessarily* so joined.

[11.5] And it is precisely in rendering rebellion liveable in this way, in conferring upon it a positivity, an ordinariness, that the predicative danger arises. For on this account, reducing Brittany to itself amounts only to placing it back upon its gnostic feet. And it is not so much that rebellion needs a firm footing, or needs to get back on its feet, whether gnostic or not, but more that it needs to reopen its wings of gnosis—that is to say... What?—to allow humans to reopen their wings. Or rather, it needs feet, but only to help it to take off, to fly away.

[11.6] Anti-philosophical angelism finds in the Canon its first wing, that of materialism; the Organon is a matter of giving it its second wing, that of gnosis.

[12.1] A gnosis is an angelic can(n)on—in the sense in which Gracq describes his arrival at the farthermost point of Cap Sizun, at the very end of the end of Brittany. 'The bus, its load now lightened, flew off like a feather to tackle the final steep climb up the plateau of the cape—back when it was still free of hotels and car parks—and suddenly, the sea that we had been skirting for a long time on our left came into view on our right, towards the Baie des Trépassés and the Pointe du Van: And that was it, my throat tightened, I felt the first stirrings of seasickness in the pit of my stomach—I became aware in a second, literally, materially, of the enormous mass of Europe and Asia behind me, *and I felt like a projectile coming out of a cannon, abruptly spat into the light.*'[66]

[12.2] The error would be to imagine that the can(n)on could be reduced to the canonical. But the author puts us on our guard immediately following his description of the experience of Brittany as gnosis or angelic can(n)on: 'I never found again, neither there nor elsewhere, that cosmic, brutal sensation of flight—intoxicating, exhilarating—which had completely taken me by surprise.'

[12.3] The opposition between the canonical and the can(n)on is as weak as its consequences are strong, the can(n)on finding in it the means to invert the characteristic signs of the canonical. As much as canonical Brittany is stable, solid, constant, a universal constant even, Brittany qua gnosis is precarious, fragile, inconstant. The canonical is regularity itself, while the can(n)on is unpredictable. Althusser developed a materialism of the encounter, also called an 'aleatory' materialism; I adopt the term in reference to Brittany considered as can(n)on, which is *aleatory gnosis*.

[12.4] The flight, the transport—in both literary and literal senses of the word—that permits gnosis—or, better, *in which gnosis consists*—is contingent, hazardous, never assured of anything, neither its advent nor its repetition. Angelic subjectivation is a grace, and as such is rare and intermittent. But to a certain extent—the extent of the institution—grace can be regularised, contingency *provoked*. And canonical Brittany is the provocation of the contingency of its can(n)on: in the mode of methodical provocation, the Two of Brittany juxtaposes the necessity of gnostic Brittany with the contingency of its gnosis.

[12.5] Brittany, archetype of the apparatus of provocation of the contingency of gnosis. Of which Armorican megalithism is perhaps the most grandiose of perversions—a splendid attempt at domestication within the context of the Neolithic revolution that was foundational for the world we live in. 'While the populations of the continent tilled and planted the soil, constructed land or lake villages,' writes Le Braz, 'Armorican humanity [...] devoted its activities to raising prestigious necropolises on its shores, large enough to receive thousands of dead—their own, of course, but probably also those of neighbouring tribes. How could the members of these tribes not have aspired to [...] be buried on the edge of the sunset, in this "lands' end", this "end of the world" which they were [...] bound to conceive as the threshold of another world [...]? By virtue of this fact, Armorica became the appointed vestibule to the afterlife, a sort of waiting room for eternity, toward which it is reasonable to think that, on fixed dates, [...] solemn processions escorted convoys of ashes and bones from all surrounding areas. To its inhabitants fell the task—well remunerated, we may suppose—of erecting the dolmens, guarding them, maintaining them, carrying out ritual libations upon them, organising the impressive ceremonies that accompanied collective burials, and finally, furnishing the army of priests and religious subalterns responsible for officiating at these sombre panegyrics: they literally lived off death'.[67]

[12.6] Breton megalithism, as brought to life vibrantly in Le Braz's archaeological speculations, might be understood as an attempt—certainly the first of which we have any traces (and what traces!)—at the socialisation of gnosis, that in which Brittany taken as can(n)on consists. Adding to the Two of Brittany, qua device of provocation of the contingency of gnosis, the Two of the making-worldly of the rebellion against the world, megalithism, at its birth on the Armorican peninsula, would be the attempt to touch what is deepest in humans by way of the collective, the building of an 'assembly-line' for the creation of a people of angels—and therefore would be a true cultural revolution whose impasse would have been commensurate with the force of its reversal into the worldly.[68]

[12.7] What I am suggesting here is the fiction, the conjecture, that the megalithic cultural revolution was the matrix—even in its very abortion—of the Neolithic revolution that is still underway today—today more than ever.

[12.8] Conjectural as it may be, the Armorican megalithic cultural revolution is itself archetypical *in its impasse*: it is the archetype of the impasse of the socialisation of rebellion. There is no rebellion—no rigorous rebellion, no rebellion that is not a pretence—that is not *solitary*, carried out by *solitary ones*. The problem of the Cultural Revolution in Cambodia, which led to horrific disaster, was certainly to have tried to overturn the world on the basis of that last point of the world that is *work*, having voided everything else; but this vicious circularity, this s(p)ecularisation of rebellion by work, which presided over the total transformation of Cambodia into a work camp, is second in the order of causes: the meticulous destruction of solitude via the destruction of the individual takes precedence over all others. In my fiction, the extreme greatness of Armorican megalithism, which makes its impasse archetypal, relates to its recourse—between the draining-out [*vidange*] of the world (pre-operated, since in fact there was hardly any world except one of sparse communities) and the angelic life [*vie d'ange*]—to the hengelic outthrust [*vit d'henge*][69] constituted by the peninsula itself, the Breton finisterre.

[12.9] A rebellion which is not mere pretence is a draining-out [*vidange*] of the world which gives rise to an angelic life [*vie d'ange*] by way of the solitary recourse to the apparatus of provocation of angelic contingency that is a finisterre, of which the hengelic outthrust [*vit d'henge*] of Brittany is the archetype. The worldly impasse of rebellion is inverted, on condition of solitude, into the angelic promontory, sometimes capable of supplying the *wings of a stasis*, of conferring upon humans the *winged stasis* which alone can stave off the flux of the worldly (and the reactive, identitarian stasis that serves as its foil).

[12.10] Draining-out, hengelic outthrust, angelic life. There is a formidable sexual element to Brittany established as gnosis or angelic can(n)on, a dimension which, moreover, is already very much present, albeit implicitly, in the writings of Gracq, beyond (or rather through) the incomparable jaculation explicitly recounted in his lines on Cap Sizun. What the author describes is Brittany's ejaculation of him. Radicalised humans, having rediscovered their wings, may enjoy the grace of being ejaculated, spat into the light by the aleatory can(n)on of a finisterre like Brittany.

[12.11] A finisterre, that is to say an encounter, a gnosis of the encounter, the organon of sailing is sexual.

[13.1] A finisterre is a generic Brittany.

[13.2] 'Finisterres—Ireland, Brittany, Galicia, Portugal, the first oceanic islands [...]. In the depths of their soul, panic', writes Eugenio d'Ors at the very end of his study on the baroque, for him the permanent category of thought that pits the human against society, and which finds one of its major representatives in Daniel Defoe's Robinson Crusoe. 'Panic, an immemorial inheritance from the time when these lands were on the edge of a sea with no known limit. One cannot occupy a front row seat in the theatre of mystery and remain immune.'[70]

[13.3] Panic no doubt, but jubilation too. The panic and jubilation appropriate to an encounter with the infinite—appropriate to the encounter *tout court*, for there is no encounter except with the other, and for finitude the only other is the infinite. A finisterre, a lands' end, is an encounter, and doubly so: both for the spectator that Ors evokes, and for the actor of whom he says nothing. A passive encounter that holds fast to the shore, at that limit of the land where the sea begins. An active encounter, that of a finitude embracing the infinite and, in embracing it, being projected into it or projecting into it those who inhabit it.

[13.4] A finisterre is an encounter, an encounter as necessity and as contingency.
On one hand, encounter as canonical necessity, since the circumscription proper to a finisterre is a separation only in so far as it is a shore—that is, an encounter with the sea. And on the other hand, encounter as contingency of the can(n)on, alea of gnosis, of being catapulted into the light.

[13.5] Finisterre, the Two, the oriented—or, better, *occidented* (with the dimension of occasionality, alea, grace, and hence of fall or failure, that envelopes the *accident* we hear echoed in the word) copresence of a necessary circumscription and a contingent opening, in which the canonical encounter and the fear it provokes make possible the can(n)on of the encounter and the jubilation in which it consists. Every angel is terrible, of course; but only for its spectator. Whereas for its actor, it is enthusiasm itself.

[13.6] An apparatus for the provocation of grace, a finisterre is a place of encounter, of tearing away from the world: a *place of joy*. And it is not by chance if the French language describes as '*lieux de joie*'[vii] those closed places which the world—that sordid open-air brothel of which practice is the whore and philosophy the grand madam—sees fit to condemn.

[13.7] On the scale of joy, Polynesia is certainly not just one finisterre among others but, along with Brittany, constitutes the other archetypal finisterre—if we are to believe Victor Segalen, in any case—and there is no reason to think he is exaggerating: 'For two years in Polynesia, joy made me sleep badly. I woke up crying with the intoxication of the dawning day.'[71] Two years of extreme joy! For an *aleatory* gnosis, that's really something. It seems that in Polynesia the angel is a marathon runner of grace.

---

vii. [*Lieu de joie*, brothel—trans].

POINT 14

[14.1] A boat is a mobile finisterre.

[14.2] What counts is not movement, but the *apparatus to which a physical movement contributes, in so far as it permits another, metaphysical, movement.* Inversely then to the thinking of the champions of movement, for whom an apparatus, whatever it may be, place or speech, only has value in movement, through movement, and for movement, and even, ultimately, as in Deleuze, Guattari, or Lyotard, through, for, and in its abolition in the name of a nomadism of intensities.

[14.3] I must of course deal with the domain of movement. But not by privileging its theoretical figureheads, whose thought innervates hegemonic spiritualism[viii] to the point of fusing with it (so that today the terms used by spiritualism and Deleuzism are to a large extent interchangeable): nothing in their work is at all consistent with my proposition, except locally, or as a negative of my research—and worse, for all too often spiritualism is a forger's thought. I approach movement instead via subjects capable of furnishing me with a material that can be made use of in spite of the logic in which it is caught up, people who attract and repel me at the same time—*so near yet so far,* as Hugues Choplin says of he and I.

[14.4] The movementism of the outside, of the dérive and the voyage, may well attack this or that figure of the world, but the fact remains that *it does not so much combat the world as aim to rediscover it,* in the guise of its primary enigma or its youth, to use terms that recur again and again, like the foam of the tide, in the books of Michel Le Bris.[72]

---

viii. [On spiritualism, see translator's note i—trans.]

[14.5] In the same way, 'it is the desire to create, or to discover, or to rediscover, a cosmos—a world of beauty and order (of chaotic order)',[73] that determines Kenneth White's approach, as advocated from the time of his first book.

[14.6] Movement, which is movement toward the world, occupies the position of a cardinal operator in contemporary thought, to the point where White, for example, can write that 'everything is in movement, all the time'. And yet he holds open a place for 'something fundamental' that would resist 'a world that is increasingly an amorphous mass of neutral localities'.[74] The place, for him, is linked to a movement that seems to be missing from the actual world. And like Le Bris, the place he has chosen above all, the place to which he has returned, having been born there, is Brittany, a 'granitic place of resistance'.[75] This resistance is not canonical, however, it is instead a resistance to that which resists movement. Making it possible to 'breathe better, live better, be there better'.[76] To this Le Bris adds a good dose of trenchancy, but what is essential is lost. And it is White himself who is the proof of it, when he reprises Gracq's words (without citing him directly): 'In my hermitage on the North Armorican coast, right in the middle of the Atlantic arc that goes from Scotland to Portugal, I have the feeling of having all of Europe behind my back, and therefore all of Asia, of which Europe is the promontory. There, I work'— I hold my breath—'among other things, on a book about Brittany: the profound Brittany, the open Brittany'.[77] A gnostic inspiration, but above all, no gnosis.

[14.7] The various modes of the 'thought of the outside' serve to articulate a gnostic material with a worldly logic. Whence their 'presence' in the real, in a certain sense, but a presence that is immediately correlated with a flight into realisation, since the real, for this thought of the outside as for spiritualism in general, exists only by way of reality. Theirs is a quest for a movement outside of all identitarian ideology, which tends toward a 'new mondialism',[78] a globalism of consciousness, beyond limited localism and abstract universalism (and its commercial trimmings), as developed by the world-literature and world-speech of a 'geopoetics'.

[14.8] Nomadism, which Kenneth White and Deleuze and Guattari make claim to and dispute over,[79] is one of the great figures of the thought of the outside. The solitary sailor clearly participates in nomadism, but it is difficult to make use of the concept given that its 'deterritorialised' terrain has become decidedly swampy ground. The distinction between movement and speed in *A Thousand Plateaus*' 'Treatise on Nomadology' must however be considered: 'a movement may be very fast, but that does not give it speed; a speed may be very slow, or even immobile, yet it is still speed. Movement is extensive; speed is intensive'. Relativity of movement, absoluteness of speed, which is absolute movement. 'It is therefore not surprising that reference has been made to spiritual voyages effected without relative movement, but in intensity, in one place: these are part of nomadism'.[80] The solitary sailor, like the nomad, is immobile, in so far as for them there can be no question of there being a beginning and end of the voyage, their having no aim other than to stay where they are, on the water, never moving except so as to stay, to have the means to stay there. And both are opposed to the rootedness in identitarian soil that gives rise to the sedentarity of the autonomous individual, master of themselves. But the solitary sailor is opposed both to the transformation of the point into a line and to the rapidity-in-place of open multiplicities: the movement of the solitary sailor is not so much absolute as radical.

[14.9] Mobile, a boat is a finisterre in the sense of the mystery evoked by Ors in the passage cited above: the very mystery in which it is inscribed, and which makes of itself a mystery.[81] 'A mystery,' as Serge Valdinoci clarifies, being 'neither a problem nor an enigma nor a rebus. The essence of the mystery is that it *devours itself as it develops*'.[82] Rooted in the sea, the boat draws its movement from itself as it advances. Again, among boats, we must distinguish between worlds and finisterres, between those which, linking together lands, effacing the all-devouring, erasing the mystery, are worlds, extensions and concentrations of the world— and those which, remaining always at the centre of the circle of the marine horizon, as formidable as their speed may be,[83] and as great a wake as they may leave behind them, are finisterres.

[14.10] The horizon is that beyond which one cannot see, but also that which allows one to see, that which conditions visibility. *Horizon* in Greek, from the verb *horizein*, to separate, to delimit, to trace out a frontier, which has the same root as *horismos*, definition. The shore is not the only trait of the finisterre; it is doubled by the horizon, the circle of the horizon, that 'circular mirror on the scale of the entire sky and sea which sends you back your own image and which you must traverse', as Jean-François Deniau writes of sailing on the high seas. The circumscription of the shore of a finisterre or of the hull of a mobile finisterre is inscribed within that of the horizon, superimposed upon it without either one dominating the other. 'In any long crossing, this is what strikes you first, and the first impression, which is the best one, also happens to be the last: the physical feeling, sometimes to the point of being oppressive, of the absolute, flawless, mathematical circle that surrounds you twenty-four hours a day and moves with you. This is what makes the long crossing nothing like, nothing *at all* like, a regatta or a cruise. In any magical evocation, the operator begins by drawing a circle. Only the long crossing is magical.' Time no longer exists, it is 'space that moves'.[84] Deniau allows the mystery he describes to exist only under the inconsistent, occult, and frivolous heading of magic. For he does not want to *know* what he has seen. Nothing is more exact or more tangible than mystery, which is the essence of sailing.

[14.11] Only finisterres sail radically, since they use space to abolish time. Ships for racing or cruising, for war or trade, for exploitation or exploration, which are nothing but a link between lands or a negation of the sea they cross, use time to abolish space: they do not so much sail as make the sea worldly.[85] What counts for the sailor is the boat, at the centre of the circle of the sea; what counts for the worldly sea user is the circle itself, in so far as it must be broken out of. Sailing traverses the circle of the sea only so as to stay within it; it breaks its circumscription only for anti-s(p)ecular ends: so as to avoid making world. Radical, sailing is a traversal, a *crossing without exit*.

[14.12] Sailing can be a crossing without exit only because it is a twofold crossing, at once active and passive. To sail is to traverse while allowing oneself to be traversed.

[14.13] To sail is both to master everything, to have a total mastery of the boat (otherwise one is headed for catastrophe, whether major or minor) and to be entirely mastered, to be totally at the mercy of an all-powerful force. Neither one nor the other nor a compromise between them: both, at the same time. There is sailing only with Two.

[14.14] The compromise between or dialectic of exercising mastery and submitting to it may suggest the dynamic of board sports. But sailing is not an affair of fluxes, of surfing the elements. If sailing shares any features with board sports, they do not relate to its essence; in fact, on the contrary, surfing is one of the greatest models of the worldly life: *to succeed in life* is to know how to support oneself upon the forces present so as to remain on the crest of the wave for as long as possible, until the next one comes along, and so on, in an acceleration with no assignable end, with no end in sight other than death. The various modes of the thinking of the outside recognise themselves in this model, to which they nevertheless make certain adjustments, being quite aware of the abomination of such 'success', starting with its completely unliveable nature. Whence the great themes of the folding of the line of the outside in Deleuze, the art of living in Foucault, concentration in White, and habitation in Le Bris.

[14.15] Circumscription is the canonical condition of sailing: its specularity. And sailing is a methodical condition of circumscription: its traversal, its crossing. Since the sea constitutes the anti-s(p)ecular mirror of melancholy, sailing may also be called the discipline of the humanisation of humans in and by way of the traversal of their essential melancholy. Crossing without exit, gnosis without salvation: an organon of radicalisation. In so far as it is at once possession and dispossession of oneself (a self extended into the finisterre that embodies it, that is its organon), sailing is pure subjectivation. The solitary sailor can be defined as the being *sovereignly dispossessed of itself.*

[14.16] *Theorrorism I* combatted sufficient s(p)ecularity and the circles of the world whose principle it is, by opposing to them the straight line, in one direction, with no turning back. But this line that breaks the circles of the world was never anything but the infinite development of worldly circularity itself. *Theorrorism I* did not exit from philosophy, but not because it had never entered it—rather because it took philosophy's ring road, mistaking it for a Route 66 of thought. *Theorrorism II* opposes to sufficient s(p)ecularity the specularity of sailing, whose movement is that of mystery: development via self-devouring, flush with the all-devouring. A specularity from before the world, in the sense that it is from *before the sufficiency that secularises specularity*.

[14.17] A radical movement, this movement of the boat which is not a link but a solitude,[86] not a world but a finisterre. A movement such that the sea is in it metaphysically rather than physically, or before being so physically. An *anti-physical* sea. In which every finisterre is immersed, including one that no drop of salt water will ever touch.[87] A sea that every finisterre sails *because, first of all, this sea itself sails*, displacing itself around the finisterre whatever it may be, mobile or immobile, artificial or natural.

POINT 15

[15.1] Anti-physical, 'the sea also sails,' as Xavier Grall observed, not as a sailor—which he was not—but as a Breton, sheltering from the storm in his Botzulan farm. 'Everything moves, I stay. Everything screams, I hold my silence. But in this upheaval, thoughts arrange themselves....' Theorem of radical movement: 'I am the seamark of my own errancy.'[88]

[15.2] Brittany, islands, peninsulas, boats.... Natural or artificial, mobile or not, a finisterre is an angelic provocation, an apparatus for the provocation via circumscription of the contingency of gnosis. A finisterre *must be invented*. It is the monastery for the monk, for whom the church is like a boat made of stone, a sonorous vessel for one who knows how to make it vibrate. But it is also, to a certain extent, *and under the strict condition of solitude*, the prison cell for the prisoner or the boarding room for the student. And also, no doubt, the stage for the actor—but in any case, never the front-row seat of the spectator.

[15.3] Provocateurs of the contingency of grace, those monks of whom Jean-Pierre Abraham speaks, consumed, as he imagines them, by envy and spite: 'I am sure that, with their way of assembling poor stones to imprison the light and make it turn, they saw God: they constrained him violently to reveal his height, and his depths, his abrupt visage. Their faith was not saccharine. The brightnesses of the dawn were triumphant.'[89] But what a provocation of the contingency of gnosis for Abraham himself is the Armen,[90] the lighthouse over which he presides until he exhausts its organon, renouncing completely, from that moment on, his profession as lighthouse keeper.

[15.4] 'I had the impression that my life was proceeding without me, and without my noticing it—so much so that, one fine day, I decided finally to make a change. I had seen the Armen, I had passed by on the boat [a minesweeper of the National Navy which he had joined during his military service], and from quite far off what's more, but all of a sudden I decided I would go there. I had truly found my place, I believe that this is what one must search for, a place where one can become oneself', explained Abraham in an improbable TV report filmed at the lighthouse at the beginning of 1962. 'For me, it has never been a question of choosing between many lighthouses, it was the Armen that I saw first, and it was the only one that interested me. When I've had enough of this place, I don't think I'll consider going to another lighthouse, it will be over. But I'm not about to leave tomorrow.'[91] It would actually be the day after tomorrow, two years later. But the exhaustion of the organon of the lighthouse had come before this, for he notes in *Armen*, in an entry dated 30 April [1963]: 'I don't think I shall write much more here.' And on 6 April, in the midst of an overwhelming oppression that sets him at a distance from himself and gives him, implicitly, the formula of sailing, the formula of mystery: 'When this passion that drives me in my work encounters within me a movement as strong as itself, but which at the same moment detaches me from it, I will be finally, torn, traversed, alive.'

[15.5] A finisterre—this is what I think Vincent La Soudière lacked throughout his life, he who wrote: 'I possess no place from which to speak. To my thought, to my consciousness, to the words I speak there corresponds no—or almost no—reality. Just like a coin that is no longer backed by gold.'[92] A finisterre, that is to say the apparatus of a two-fold traversal each side of which he knew better than anyone, but isolated one from the other, separated, drifting in the 'cloaca' of the world. 'To know is to traverse. To love is to allow oneself to be traversed', he observes in his notes just a few years before his suicide. Without having the right means at his disposal to draw the conclusion: to sail is to traverse while allowing oneself to be traversed.[93] And of course, perhaps he would have still killed himself in some finisterre. But certainly not for the same reasons.

[15.6] Why do so few *sail*? Conrad says it, and Éric Tabarly, a great reader of Conrad, after him: because sailing is an activity that doesn't suit impostors well.[94] But La Soudière was anything but an impostor, indeed he was one of the greatest exemplars of probity I know of. 'I am a dark and high galley whose chained rowers are my thoughts and desires. This is why the galley hastens toward the enemy's spur that will disembowel it',[95] he set down, as a way of saying—as a Breton despite himself—*kentoc'h mervel eget em zaotra*, 'rather death than defilement'. Except that there is death and then there is death. And not all deaths have the same status. And Breton, finisterrian, marine death—for the sea is still Breton[96]—is not the worldly death always already chosen by La Soudière.

[15.7] There is a death that is not the enemy, but which also sails, and it is finisterrian death.

POINT 16

[16.1] Sailing has a great deal in common with death. Not in the sense that to sail is to risk death, drowning at sea, although such a risk does exist, especially when sailing alone;[97] but in the sense, indicated by a rhetorical question of Bachelard's,[98] that Death is the first sailor.

[16.2] There is worldly death, coextensive with the life of the world whose underside, nerve, and last recourse it is: the permanent possibility of escaping the world that makes life indefinitely bearable. Thus Cioran, a model of the genre, whose life a suicidal bent grasped in thought may not have saved but at least safeguarded, such that it continued on into a senility ravaged by illness. Thus Lacan, haranguing his audience: 'Death is in the domain of faith. You are quite right to believe that you are going to die, of course; it keeps you going. If you didn't believe that, could you bear the life you have? If you couldn't rely so solidly on that certainty that it will end, could you bear this tale?'[99] The dialectical counter-worldliness of worldly death.

[16.3] There is finisterrian death, which sails, and constitutes the archetype of the solitary sailor. Not counter-worldly, that is to say counter-erotic (Eros being the principle of the bond from which the world is woven) but *anti-erotic*, finisterrian death is the death that vivifies and traverses Perros: 'Unbridled taste for failure. For death. For a certain death. Which disposes me to a frantic taste for life. So long as it demands nothing of me. If I play, I am afraid of winning.'[100] The anti-erotics of sailing delivers a life that is not a bond but a solitude.

[16.4] The anti-erotics of sailing is the *herethical* discipline that follows from Anacharsis's theorem: 'There are the living, the dead, and those who go to sea.'[101] To sail is to be neither living nor dead but both at once, without any unity of contraries or coincidence of opposites. It is to hold the Two of death and life, to hold fast in the jaws of life and of death, flush to that which develops only by devouring itself. To live from being dead.

[16.5] Thanks to herethics one is not condemned to the void by refusing the world, and one is not condemned to the world by refusing the void. Sailing—radical, fully human work—consists in seeking and holding, via incessant adjustments, the *right distance*: far enough from the world not to be sucked in and crushed, close enough not to fall into the void (or into the illusion of having vanquished the void, when one has not only renewed it but extended it to create a world of one's own).

[16.6] The anti-erotics of sailing cannot be said to be an endorsement of life unto death. For it does not 'approve' of life any more than it does of death: it *is* life, qua death at work, qua organon of death. And if it gives onto a certain jouissance, it is that of solitude, not that of a desire renewed indefinitely only to see its object always slipping away into the province of death.

[16.7] In the jouissance of solitude, the body itself is a finisterre. The self of which sailing is at once possession and dispossession may be the self extended into the boat or into any finisterre that embodies it, that is its organon; but it is also the self reduced to its physical body, the jouissance of which is that of a subject that never feels 'so much a subject as when it is an object', as Goldschmidt writes, reading Rousseau; 'it is the same, the perpetual desire for the perfect circle, the specular jouissance of self by self. And it is from this that it can draw its *proof*: exclusively founded on this pleasure of being self. As if turned back upon it and yet issuing from it, it is his own body that Rousseau desires: women are an extension of it; strangely, they are a mirror of it'.[102]

[16.8] For Rousseau women are the extension of his body of solitude, just as the boat—itself taken as feminine in English, a language which has the maritime rigour to say *she* rather than *it*—is the institution of the solitary sailor. The good boat, writes Yvon Le Corre, is 'like a mirror of oneself'.[103]

Jean-Pierre Abraham superimposes the two dimensions, those of sailing and the jouissance of solitude: 'I do not yet have in me the mixture of recklessness and nerve necessary to sail well. One day, surely, I will be on a boat once more, plunging deep into the waves. To be on the sea with a girl, there's nothing better.'[104] One might point out, of course, that he does not identify the boat with the girl, and after all, he went on to marry; and yet the formula, including what it contains of the undecidable, is a just and exact one.

[16.9] Regardless of orientation, gender identity, and practices (registers which should not be confused, or else one will understand nothing, and nothing of oneself to start with), *sex is a form of solitary sailing, that is to say a sailing with two, like the sailor and the boat*; a way of exercising a dispossessed sovereignty. Thus, in Mathieu Riboulet's *Le Corps des anges* I read: 'There he learned the elementary rules of the courtesy of bodies, the endless variations of pleasure, how one can make oneself an object without ever renouncing oneself as subject—all weapons that would be of great use to him throughout the years to follow. The lesson of bodies is like the lesson of the dead, it endows with enormous force those who indulge it without restraint.'[105] The organon of sailing, sexual, is anti-erotic, its jouissance an aleatory jouissance untouched by happiness—that is to say, capable of abolishing the very category.[106] 'And long memory on the sea for a nation of Lovers in arms!'[107]

[17.1] To be alone is to be not one, but two. Just as to be two is not to be many. Solitude is only rebellion against the world as two, in the Two. The One, to which every-one relates or through which they are determined, is the world, its point of fusion, synonymous with the pulverulence of the Multiple. The curse of the existence of the many. To which it is a question of opposing not individual solitude, the citadel of the One, but the solitude of the subject, the grace and labour of the Two.

[17.2] The solitary sailor is alone with their boat. *Alone with*, alone *because* with. To embark as a solitary sailor is to be two, to form a Two with your vessel: at once inseparable and separate. 'Those who don't know that a sail is a living being will never understand anything about boats or about the sea',[108] as the companion of *Joshua*, Bernard Moitessier, remarks. A living being of the Two that it forms with the solitary sailor.

[17.3] A boat that does not act as a bond is a solitude, and an organisation of solitude. Solitude of two, of the Two; and organon—finisterrian method and body—of sailing.

[17.4] What goes for the canon of circumscription goes for the organon of sailing, which is divided into the two aspects of the double genitive. Taken subjectively, it is the organon *that constitutes sailing*, that is of its essence: it is the body and the method of the twofold traversal that is sailing. Taken objectively, it is the organon which the twofold traversal that is sailing *constitutes*, the body and method that arise from sailing, and order the sailor's existence.

[17.5] To sail is to make a boat serve one's purposes, but above all to serve the purposes of the boat, to place oneself in its service, so that it can—not so much render the service expected of it, since it is not a matter of give and take—but be what it is capable of being, namely, the finisterre without which there is nothing for humans but the world. And so, to sail is always to put the boat before oneself.

[17.6] Regularising silence and solitude on the sea by breaking them, the can(n)on of circumscription allows one to think, to begin thinking again, to exit from the brutalising effects of finitude while remaining flush with the infinite. Materialising and making fruitful the can(n)on of circumscription, the organon of sailing is thought in act—that which continually begins again to think without ever being sure it is truly thinking. If the canon is the starter, if it restarts thought, then the organon is the motor, that which thinks, thought being nothing other than its own restarting, aleatory, rare, and intermittent.

[17.7] But what would one not do in order to think. 'Thought only thinks by not thinking, that is what makes things last', writes Emmanuelle Rousset.[109] 'This is where the extreme closedness, the sweet closedness of rites becomes necessary,' responds Jean-Pierre Abraham. This is where ritual, 'the thinking of hours, the table of service, our humble benefactors', becomes necessary. 'Like the hours that provide the rhythm for the life of monks. Discrete points of support in order, slowly and surely, without any grand gesture, to get to the end of bad days':[110] to await thought, and joy. This is where ritual becomes necessary, the subjectivated repetition that is the objective organon.

POINT 18

[18.1] The organon of sailing taken in the objective genitive—ritual, the tool of waiting—draws its being from the sea, which is, as Perros's verse has it, 'extraordinarily monotonous / Like everything important.'[111]

[18.2] A boat, qua finisterre, is an angelic can(n)on, an attack on the sufficiency of the world. But an aleatory can(n)on, an apparatus which encompasses a set of rituals that allow one to await grace without sinking, without abandoning oneself to the world. A routine which no-one has described better than Conrad: 'It is a great doctor for sore hearts and sore heads, too, your ship's routine, which I have seen soothe—at least for a time—the most turbulent of spirits. There is health in it, and peace, and satisfaction of the accomplished round; for each day of the ship's life seems to close a circle within the wide ring of the sea horizon. It borrows a certain dignity of sameness from the majestic monotony of the sea. He who loves the sea loves also the ship's routine.'[112]

[18.3] Those gestures that are unavoidable—laundry, or cleaning,[113] a nice tweet featuring a well-turned phrase or an image of beautiful light,[114] an impeccable manoeuvre, a clean course, drawing a long trace on the water and on the map—just to keep oneself afloat *while waiting*. To give oneself ritual or daily habit as a kind of rope-cutter for the nets of the world, one that can protect you from worldliness only because it is waiting to reopen its wings. Subjectively, the organon of sailing is attack; objectively, it is an 'active, pulsing wait'.[115]

[18.4] Ritualised, methodical waiting protects one from the world only because it prepares the attack, and it only prepares the attack because it is already in itself a kind of attack, an attack both *minoritarian* and *undermining*: because it is already alive and vibrating with the attack that it is preparing. Waiting avoids being resolved into a banal worldly passivity if and only if of itself it is already an attack on the world. And this underminoring attack of waiting owes its force to the *provocation* of the contingency of the angelic attack that is enveloped in ritual, even in its failure.

[18.5] Those who imagine it is possible to succeed. Those who believe that one can only fail. And those who know that there is success only in failure. (Radical failure, which is the cipher of the soul, not the failure that would be a condition of success in so far as one overcomes it. The soul, that is, according to Cioran's definition: 'everything in us that refuses to participate in the world. An unlimited communion with oneself. It finds its raison d'être in auto-devouring, and could not be anything other than its own cannibal.'[116] Which is to say: that which is *animated* by mystery.) There is grace in failure.

[18.6] The institution of the *place* wards off the return of the world in the place of the void that the sea delivers. The method of *ritual* saves from itself the thought that only thinks by not thinking, the thought which, in order not to think, reflects,[117] by inscribing its specularity within the very life of the soul that it allows it to become, nourishing it upon itself, upon its own empty repetition. Ritual saves thought from being swallowed up in its emptiness via the animation of life, albeit a bloodless animation.[118] (Bloodless life, you know? When you're sucked out from within and remain empty, full of yourself).

[18.7] The *place* is the last word of anti-politics, *ritual* the last word of anti-erotics.

[19.1] Articulating anti-erotics within an anti-politics, *ports* give rise to the method of waiting that is ritual.

The ultimate form of waiting-place, a port is the sojourn of souls par excellence, a human sojourn. A port, an airlock between land and sea, *a little quarter made of the same stuff as the world* (since without commerce, in both narrow and broader senses, it would not exist) is by virtue of this already *like a quarter of the soul sunken in self-sufficiency*. 'It is in a port, Ougarit, that the alphabet was born. And from it, writing and all of literature', Charles Madézo observes. 'We should not be surprised, then, at the strange resonances between the soul and the architecture of ports.'[119] A writer of the sea and an engineer of public works who built harbour structures, Madézo knows what he's talking about. As does one of the ship's mates Conrad knew during his maritime career, for whom '[p]orts are no good: ships rot, men go to the devil'.[120] When waiting s(p)ecularises and, losing itself, sets up camp, raises the big top of the great circus of the world, tourism, sport, transport, and commercialisations of all kinds, we can indeed speak then of rot and vice.

[19.2] Ports are the only possible sustainable places of sojourn for the solitary sailor. A sustainable sojourn—that is to say, a working one, embedded in economic life.

Ports and work have a common structure, in which subjectivation is the only guiding thread, as an antidote to subjection and desubjectivation, rot and vice. So working in a port, which means nothing more than working for a port, organising and defending a place of waiting, a radical sojourn, can serve as an occasional mode of the work of being human.

[19.3] All work that is not a mode of radical work is prostitution—sex work, the most reviled of all, being the least contemptible by far.

[19.4] The generic prostitution that is worldly work is only so widely accepted, so seldom challenged, because the worldly are so bored with their lives (cf. 5.11): they need to be *occupied*. To slide from that to accepting or even championing *employment* (or employing oneself, in the case of the entrepreneur), even beyond the satisfaction of economic needs, only requires a little lubricant. Work—*the fact of being employed, of treating oneself as a slave according to the dispositions, inherited from Roman law, that found the contract of work*—is the living suicide of the cowardly and the apotheosis of moronic stupidity—those who were already so and those upon whom work has worked to make them so.

[19.5] The triad of the labour market, human resources, and employability that lies at the heart of the metaphysics of management derives its authority not so much from the efficiency of the shitheads who implement it as from the idiocy of those who object to it despite not being equipped with any metaphysical horizon whatsoever. Beneath its buffoonish exterior, management is no laughing matter: it is a great philosophy, the philosophy of a world finally freed from the abyss. (We know what *Moby Dick* has to say about the soul: 'Anything down there about your souls? [...] Oh! Perhaps you hav'n't got any [...]. No matter though, I know many chaps that hav'n't got any,—good luck to 'em; and they are all the better off for it. A soul's a sort of fifth wheel to a wagon.')[121] A world finally without soul, and without that which animates souls—finally efficient, or in short: *the* world as such, finally *realised*.

[19.6] The world has no outside (there is no other world) and no alternative (there is no world that is otherwise): there is only the doublet of unlimited commercialisation and of management as metaphysics of a humanity delivered from the abyss, reduced to a puddle of anthropological ennui to be absorbed by the Market. Except that one cannot deliver oneself from the abyss.

[19.7] Lean on the abyss. Do not start from the world, even from its nullity as nihilism does, in order to detach yourself from the world. Inscribe the consistency of rebellion in the very void itself, in the very radical inconsistency to which the human holds, lose yourself in it—for otherwise the world will always have won by serving as a support for that which refuses it. And the abyss, it grows by devouring itself. It is a matter of working flush with the abyss. Of failing: of holding fast to the real, not yielding to reality.

[19.8] The metaphysicians of management, competitors, entrepreneurs, men of power, influence, or money, each one often a motley assortment of all the above, are devotees of a success which is not even a misguided quest for an absolute, since it has no source, no motor, other than jealousy of the success of others and the desire to feel that others are jealous of one's success.[122] Since they are unable to receive criticism except as itself a pure manifestation of jealousy for what they are, what they have, or what they do, any idea of distinguishing between human emulation and worldly competition is radically inaccessible to them, as is the idea of establishing the human, nothing but human economic regime that is *simplicity, beyond wealth and poverty.*

[19.9] It is incredible that simplicity should be conflated with poverty, thus making the accumulation of wealth the norm of what is wanted and desired, when wealth and poverty are equally criminal. It is a matter of attaining simplicity, that is to say of having everything one needs without having too much of anything, nothing superfluous. No other economic objective than simplicity, as antidote to the capital mode of the dissolution of humans into the world formed by the couplet of poverty and wealth. As distant from poverty as it is from wealth, simplicity alone is human, nothing but human. To escape from simplicity is not only to enter into the world (whose walls are held up by the couplet of wealth and poverty); it is no more or less than to exit from humanity. What makes one fall out of simplicity onto the side of wealth or poverty is becoming-worldly: the destruction of humans. For anti-economic simplicity comes from before poverty and wealth.

[19.10] The only property that is really needed—but radically so—is that which extends and immediately protects the body, not as (making-worldly) prosthesis but as (subjectivating) institution. As far as wealth is concerned, any more property than this is criminal, as is the lack of this radical property, since it spells poverty.

[19.11] These elements of an anti-economics intersect with Jacques Fradin's 'simple way of rebellion' (even if his anti-economics, superb in its meticulous violence, remains, to my knowledge, critical or genealogical, with no positivity apart from that of its effectuation as non-economics, a positivity that itself is somewhat doubtful) along with the work of Pierre Legendre, Alain Supiot, and Alain Deneault. They lie at the heart of my Project of a constitution for Brittany.

[19.12] The last words of Alain Deneault's *Politics of the Extreme-Centre* are 'Radicalise yourselves!'[123] I'm not so sure that radicalisation can be the object of a slogan, as engaging as it might be. Except in the case of worldly radicalisation, which refuses the world by refusing the human in the same gesture: terrorism is the fulfilment of this nihilist radicalisation. Whereas pure radicalisation refuses the world by refusing to give the human over to the world: its theorrorism, which with a beating of its wings attacks the world, also attacks terrorism, to which it is the sole antidote.

[19.13] If 'radicalisation' is a murderous reaction to mass desubjectivation,[124] the problem is not to 'deradicalise' but to make available paths of real radicalisation. That is to say, anti-philosophical paths. This is what the progressivism of worldly radicals, who like to play at being the smartest even when they are at their wits' end, sometimes pretends to understand.[125]

[20.1] Against the historical eternalisation of the world machined by sufficient s(p)ecularity, it is a question, as I say in 8.14 in agreement with Saint-Pol-Roux, of 'putting the serpent's tail in its mouth: posthistory–prehistory': a short-circuiting of the world (of the time of the world or of world as time) of which Brittany is the place. The place, canonical, gnostic, but also the means, organonic: the gnosis. Constant, necessary place and aleatory, contingent means, generalised as finisterre. Or, more precisely, place and means *genericised* as finisterre, an apparatus which endows anti-philosophy with its full positivity.

[20.2] To inhabit a finisterre, or rather, in keeping with place and ritual, to *habituate oneself to inhabiting a finisterre*, is to equip oneself with an organon of the end of the world, a theory and method of solving the problem posed to life by the world. The theory of the solitary sailor is the organisation of a specularity that short-circuits sufficient s(p)ecularity, and in which the problem of life finds, as a solution, a life that is— What, 'without problems'?[126] No, but *without questions* (see note 10). A life in which thought would be life, in which the Two of life and thought would be such that the abstract would reenter into the concrete, would be a wedge driven into it. So the world can do little harm to the solitary sailor, for they already carry within themselves their whole tragedy. It may bother them, it may frustrate them. It may kill them. That's all.[ix]

[20.3] The tragedy lies not so much in failure as in the gnosis of failure, the subjectivated knowledge that one always fails but that failure, the fall, can be a grace. This is the 'wings raised to the second power' of which Simone Weil speaks, the wings that 'can make things come down without weight'.[127]

---

ix. [From the phrase spoken by Alain Delon in *Nouvelle Vague* (dir. J.-L. Godard, 1990), taken from Jacques Chardonne's *L'Amour c'est beaucoup plus que l'amour* (Paris: Albin Michel, 1957, republished 1992): '*Une femme ne peut pas beaucoup nuire à un homme. Il porte en lui-même toute sa tragédie. Elle peut le gêner, l'agacer. Elle peut le tuer. C'est tout*'—trans.]

[20.4] For humans, there is only the world—except that there is solitude. And solitude comes *before*. Whence anti-philosophy, which precedes the world-thought that is philosophy, and determines how it is
traversed. Anti-philosophy is not *another* philosophy, a philosophy that
would be 'human' (a terminological misunderstanding which non-philosophy, in the absence of a logic of Two, takes to the entirely rhetorical
heights of the oxymoron), but *radical independence from philosophy,
that is to say sovereign traversal of all philosophy*. For humans there is
only melancholy without cause and without limit, and the pain of being
in the world—except that there is the joy that their traversal procures.
That's all there is: awaiting the joy that attacks the world. And then *holding fast* in that waiting, making it a provocation to attack: regularising
gravity, to provoke the grace that will volatilise it.

[20.5] To navigate melancholy—that is, to reject both the inanity of bon
vivants (and even those who 'live life to the full', proclaiming 'Melancholy? Oh, I don't have time for that') and the cynicism of living suicides.
No wisdom, except stultification. But perhaps a sanctity without God
and without salvation, a nothing but human, *melancholeric* sanctity,

Many of my sentences are silently détourned quotes from elsewhere, including this one. Some in spite of myself and discovered after the fact, most deliberate. Apart from one exception, which was not an inventive détournement but a theft, albeit an involuntary one, I have not indicated their origin.

My text is punctuated by a great many citations. There are several potential explanations for this, principal among them, I think, the one given by Jean Starobinski to Robert Burton: 'The author, when he wants to speak in a more striking way, speaks in the voice of others. He [...] speaks himself through the text of the masters, which he détourns to his own uses. [...] The extent of the recourse to citation, in an author who declares himself melancholy, invites us once more to ask ourselves about the relation between melancholy and the perpetual insertion of a borrowed discourse within one's own discourse. If on one hand there is here an attestation of knowledge, there is also, on the other hand, an admission of 'insufficiency' [...] [of] melancholy consciousness: it needs supports, external contributions [...]. It fills itself with foreign substance in order to fill its own void.'[128]

From the moment I first started to write it, years ago, I composed this book directly with a *finished* page layout, constrained in all dimensions: the compactness and balance of lines, paragraphs, pages, the position on each line of the last character of a paragraph....[x] (Just as, on Twitter,[129] I make it a point of honour not to publish anything that doesn't include the maximum allowed number of characters per tweet, and not one less). This constraint, echoing the formal exigency of the text, lends its enunciation a *minerality* that reinforces its lapidary—and Breton—character.[130]

---

x. [Cleaving as closely as possible to this precise and deliberate arrangement, the English translation inevitably departs from it at many points—trans.]

The words of silence articulated in this theory of the solitary sailor are theorems of an anti-biography: of a traversal of the self by the I. The self is that which tells its story and makes world; the I is that which comes before the self and traverses it. More than this: the I is that which, unless it traverses the self, will drown in it. Anti-biographical,[131] that is to say maintaining both that it is obscene to speak of oneself and that it is only about oneself that one can speak (major premise: I can only speak of myself; minor premise: to speak of myself is obscene; conclusion: I must speak of that which, in me, is not me, and yet drives me), this book is a traversal of the self by a writing *in I*.

Among the numerous notes that have been ejected to the end of this volume, and to which this coda also serves as an introduction, the reader will find, alongside technical points and scholia (in some cases more worthwhile than their pretext), most of the arguments that directly fuel the anti-biographical vein of the book. None of this is dispensable, though— that would be the last straw in such a small book.

Hardly even a book, in fact, or else a book-trap set to scuttle itself and sabotage all others. An anti-book.

Perhaps the reception of this anti-book will be altered by the global COVID-19 pandemic and the confinement and 'social distancing' measures taken almost everywhere across the planet, and which in some senses resonate with its themes. Possibly not, though, since circumscription in the context of a health crisis is most likely distinct from any rigorous solitude. And yet some have gained a sense of the idea of a *community of solitudes*, which—a small cause with major consequences— allows me to make my dedication positive: To those among the confined who found themselves humanised by lockdown.

NOTES

1. J.-J. Rousseau, *Reveries of the Solitary Walker* (London: Penguin Classics, 2004), 'Fifth Walk', 81 [translation modified].

2. My boat is a Globe-flotteur 33, designed by Michel Joubert and Bernard Nivelt, made of thick zinc-coated aluminium with a Strongall® skin in the Prometa shipyard in Tarare. Delivered in 1983, she is the third in a series that began with *Voyage*, which belonged to the French pop singer, writer, engineer, and sailor Antoine. With the experience of several years sailing on board *Om*, a Damien II that proved too large for his taste, mainly because of the maintenance it required, Antoine was looking for a smaller boat (which turned out to be a little too small in the end; he felt he had finally reached the right size with his third boat, the catamaran *Banana Split*, to which he has remained faithful for thirty years). I am the sixth owner. For the record, her previous owner took the opposite tack to Antoine, trading up from the Globe-flotteur to a Damien II.

She's a good boat. A good companion. Not a 'beautiful' boat, perhaps, but a simple, sober one, with a face and a personality. Possibly, if I had the means, I would have had a slightly different boat built, more individual, optimised for the use I make of it; but all of the principal defining features would remain the same.

A great many details about the Globe-flotteur 33 can be found in two of Antoine's books, the tale *Voyage aux Amériques* (Paris: Arthaud, 1986) and the technical guide *Mettre les voiles* (Paris: Arthaud, 1983, third revised and updated edition 2010), and also in Jean-Michel Sautter's *Mer des Hommes* (Louviers: L'Ancre de Marine, 2007), the story of a world tour via the Panama canal and the Cape of Good Hope, made between 2000 and 2004 with family and friends as crew, by the man who was at the time the (third) owner of the boat that is now mine.

3. As a subjectivated genre, adhered to internally and endowed with a rigour all its own, rather than a genre characterised externally, that is to say denigrated or at least explicitly placed within the constricting perspective of philosophy's range of dubious sub-products.

4. In *Déclarer la gnose. D'une guerre qui revient à la culture* (Paris: L'Harmattan, 2002), my first and until now my only sole-authored book, I announced a second volume to come, *Établir la gnose. De l'Ange qui vient à la théorie*, which in the end never appeared, at least as a published book. It does exist in another form, being present as part of 'Introduction à une gnose rigoureuse', my doctoral thesis defended at the end of 2002. Less a book proper than a collection of texts (many of which had been or have since been published elsewhere), it required a major overhaul which was put on hold during the founding, with François Laruelle and Ray Brassier, of the Organisation non-philosophique internationale (Onphi), conceived as a body for the promotion and high-intensity development of our research, a collective attempt to materialise theory. Now, the failure of Onphi, which was dissolved at the beginning of 2006 (and refounded in the aftermath on a very worldly basis) was a sign of the impasse reached on the path I had envisaged for the second part of my thesis, and the abandonment of any plan to get a book out of it. Even so, the sullied title of the second part of my phantom diptych (a triptych, in fact, since an adventurous third part, announced under the title of *La Gnose de Tintin*, was supposed to complete and recapitulate the apparatus set out in the first two) remains perfectly apt, its subtitle announcing the core of my work, expressed more rigorously here—as manifest in the formula to which this note is attached.

5. A book does not need to be written in order to exist, writing it just allows it to be read. What a book needs is an idea in the strong sense, an idea embodied and attested to in the ultra-compact materiality of a title which announces that idea in its entirety—the dual of a finitude and an infinity. In this sense, this book has existed since early 2007. A stuttering writing process, all glorious advances, pitiful setbacks, paragraphs feverishly constructed by day and joyfully trashed by night (or the other way around), and stumblings (where the only thing gained is the benevolent illusion that work is underway[a]—but perhaps I'm past the age where one celebrates the idea of constantly working?) and bittersweet paralyses, to the point where I considered abandoning the whole thing.

A *forfeit* upon which Robin Mackay, who since 2007 has constantly encouraged this work, was able to make me backtrack. My thanks to him, for this and all the rest.

(a) The late Wittgenstein offers an almost systematic account of this illusion, best summed up in the 1948 note for the preface of *Philosophical Investigations*: 'Only every so often does one of the sentences I am writing here make a step forward; the rest are like the snipping of the barber's scissors, which he has to keep in motion so as to be able to make a cut with them at the right moment.' L. Wittgenstein, *Culture and Value*, ed. G.H. von Wright with H. Nyman, tr. P. Winch (Chicago: University of Chicago Press, 1980), 66c.

6. 'Writing is a fine thing, because it combines the two pleasures of talking to yourself and talking to a crowd'. C. Pavese, *This Business of Living: Diaries 1935–1950* (London and New York Routledge, 2017), 276 (4 May 1946). It is certainly quite possible to combine these four postures of the dedication in various ways.

7. Y. Elléouët, *Falc'hun* (Paris: Gallimard, 1976), 66—a book which, alongside *Livre des rois de Bretagne* (Paris: Gallimard, 1974), makes up a great diptych of Breton gnosis, of a gnosis *without salvation*.

8. Translated as *The Paths of the Sea*, tr. P. O'Brian (New York: Harper-Collins, 1977), 295–97 [translation modified].

9. G. Lardreau, *La Mort de Joseph Staline. Bouffonnerie philosophique* (Paris: Grasset, 1978), 85.

10. The question calls for a response which, far from doing away with it, making it disappear as the solution to a problem is meant to do, instead constitutes its displacement and its renewal. The question is nourished by its response, which therefore serves as fuel for its eternalisation, the renewal being endless—without any last term that may be defined, nor any finality other than that of enabling the question to perpetuate itself.

To evoke the question is therefore not so much to illustrate s(p)ecularity metaphorically as to identify a central operator of the regime of thought which *makes world* under the authority of the Principle of Sufficient S(p)ecularity—namely, philosophy, or whatever stands in for it.

11. I introduced the notion of theorrorism [*théorisme*] in 'Prolégomènes à la rébellion comme théorisme' (DEA dissertation, Paris-Nanterre University, 1996). Although unfortunately the homophony does not work so well in English, this term, almost untouched before I used it (the *Trésor de la langue française* cites just two occurrences, which are rather lazy, in Chateaubriand and Vigny) has constituted the guiding thread of my journey for a quarter of a century now. A heterogeneous thread, however. For no doubt we must distinguish between two ages of theorrorism, with the academic year 2006–2007 constituting the hinge between them. The first type of theorrorism, which we might call 'Theorrorism I', was what led me to give up sailing; the second type of theorrorism, the new wave, which we might call 'Theorrorism II', was what started me sailing again. 'The aim being,' as I said in 2011, 'to continue [my] work by other means, those afforded me by the sailboat instituted as body or *organon* of theory' (<https://www.matiere.org/auteurs_/grelet-gilles/>).

12a. Three planes, or more exactly three irregular, uneven surfaces, each supporting a quadripartite set, are superimposed here, their hollows and protrusions combining in a play of tight determinations between levels and within each level, each quadripartite set also being oriented according to a fourth term and corresponding term by term with the other quadripartite sets. To this triple of quadruples (making-worldly, radical making-worldly, worldly radicalisation and radicalisation; philosophy, hypo-philosophy, counter-philosophy and anti-philosophy; conservatism, progressivism, nihilism, and angelism) we can add at least one more level, which supports the quadripartite set of theoreticism, tourism, terrorism—or rather terrori(ci)sm—and theorrorism. Only the third plane is labelled, for lack of any illuminating categories that might be attached to the other three. (And what is more: its category, that of ideology, does not so much clarify its content as its content clarifies it, avoiding its reduction to a subaltern and illusory mode of thought).

12b. Contrary to the quadripartite set of 'Theorrorism I', that of 'Theorrorism II' has no place for non-philosophy. Something that owes less to theorrorism than to the becoming of non-philosophy itself, as it passes from the opening up and investigation of a new continent of thought under the at once genial and obstinate impetus of François Laruelle, to a crystallisation as the strictly personal oeuvre of Laruelle—an systematic oeuvre that concludes with 'non-standard philosophy', that is to say philosophy *tout court*. Where does non-philosophy stand within the quadruple of philosophy, hypo-philosophy, counter-philosophy, and anti-philosophy? It is not a supernumerary term, but that which, within this quadruple, will have played all four roles, occupied all of the places over the course of its sequences, a *tour de force* giving rise not so much to a Reformation of philosophy as to *a* reformed philosophy, which, with *Tétralogos* (Paris: Cerf, 2019), segues into a baublisation of thought.

13. Saint-Pol-Roux, 'Litanies de la solitude', in *La Besace du solitaire*, ed. J. Goorma and A. Whyte (Mortemart: Rougerie, 2000), 51.

14. J.-C. Milner, 'Universality in Splinters', tr. P.-H. Monot, *Critical Inquiry* 46:1 (Autumn 2019). On this point as on others, I now find myself in complete opposition to an author who was long an infallible guide toward a radicality into which he himself barely ventures, but whose pathways he is able to map out like no other.

15. 'It was killing him with its silence and loneliness, making everything ordinary too beautiful to bear', writes Ken Cosgrove, under his nom de plume Dave Algonquin, at the end of season 5 episode 5 of *Mad Men* (dir. Matthew Weiner, AMC, 2007–2015).

16. Xavier Grall was also forty years old when he left Paris to go and live in Brittany. The coincidence seems significant to me. But not because

this age, being that of midlife, prompts one to take stock and perhaps to make changes in one's existence so as to best profit from the time remaining: this managerial and touristic vision of human things, not just miserable but actually *false*, was not Grall's, and is not mine either. More radically, I found that it was at forty years old that I started to live. When you're young, unless you're a moron, you mostly want to die. When you're older, things are no longer so clear. Since I entered my forties, I am *living*. No management of life, in Grall's or in my work; but a *relation of life* (as Saint-Just says of the relation of justice or Sylvain Lazarus of the relation to the real). And doubtless here there is, in the contemporary field, a shared subjective structure.

17. In support of an assertion that hardly needs corroboration, recent events whisper to me the words spoken by Victor Hugo upon his return from exile on 5 September 1870: 'Saving Paris means more than saving France, it means saving the world. For Paris is the very centre of humanity. Paris is the sacred city. Whoever attacks Paris attacks en masse the whole human species. Paris is the capital of civilisation, which is neither a kingdom nor an empire, and which is the human genre entire in its past and in its future. And do you know why Paris is the city of civilisation? Because Paris is the city of Revolution.' (Speech cited on 10 January 2016 during an official tribute to the victims of the Paris attacks of January and November 2015.)

18. The welcome afforded to humans by the world is a capital point. This welcome is neither a luxury nor a virtue. For what is the world if not the general flow of the making-worldly of humans? Being nothing but the transformation of humans into agents of the eternalisation of its own worldliness via the s(p)ecular doublet of creation and procreation, the least the world can do for itself, in its own interests, is to welcome them, to furnish them with a place. The welcoming of humans by the world is not a 'grace' granted especially to them, as an exception to a general rule of exclusion; it is much rather an essential consequence of the great principle of the world, that without which it would collapse in on itself like a soufflé.

The world is not 'capable' of welcome, it is welcoming through and through.

So what does it mean for the world to offer a warm welcome to humans? To allow them maximal development, a flourishing as complete as possible, in all respects. Religions, philosophies, and doctrines of human rights have all laid out the conditions for this. And this is what the world lives off. The development, conformation, accumulation, and realisation of humans is making-worldly itself. There is nothing human in it: it is the world and nothing but the world that lives off and survives on humans having as accomplished a life as possible (the category of 'happiness' being the worldly category par excellence). When the world puts a brake on its warm welcoming of humans, it hinders its own development, to the point of scuttling itself. And yet this is the path it almost always takes, apparently working to scuttle itself.

The damage done is generally only local, though, and is compensated for elsewhere. Strategic victory implies accepting tactical defeats. But the strategic point of view must be upheld—which obviously was the role of the Church in the West for the last thousand years. What with the Industrial Revolution and its uncontrolled aftermath, one may doubt, in spite of the successful fabrication over some decades of a limitless middle class, how far along the road to global self-destruction the world of globalisation really is. Humans exist radically only to defend themselves from the world. This is already a complex affair. We need institutions, which (to anticipate what will be detailed below) are always fragile, apparatuses of independence—like a boat, for instance—that make the unliveable liveable. But what could it mean to refuse the world when, for its part, in its own way, the world refuses itself? Perhaps this is the full meaning of the words in Kafka's *Journal*: 'In your struggle between yourself and the world, side with the world.'

19. My library is without doubt the only thing that I miss from my life on land. Some days I constantly feel its absence, whether to support a work in progress or to allow one of those free wanderings whose fruitfulness is well proven. And yet I am not totally bereft. In addition to a fairly

extensive digital library, which is invaluable both in the absence of and as a supplement to a physical library—the power of a search engine to explore a text that one already knows is unparalleled—I do indeed have an onboard library which, however limited and difficult to access it may be (since the books are all protected from water in plastic bags, shoehorned into boxes or bags which themselves are wedged into pigeonholes under seats or behind the backs of benches), nonetheless amounts to several hundred volumes. And I modify the contents of this collection periodically by exchanging books with my onshore library.

20. Appalling, if quite in keeping with the emptiness of its proclamations, all fabricated on the basis of a pedagogy whose sources are resolutely desubjectivated and desubjectivating, this jargon of the FFV, an organisation where the soul of Glénans (the soul, yes, the very soul!) was drowned at the turn of the 1990s. Having at the time just obtained my federation qualification as a trainer of yachting instructors, I experienced this drowning at close quarters, believing that I could deal with it with the means at hand—those that I was beginning to develop and those, above all, that were concealed within Glénans's own thinking, or what it I found in it.

21. J.-P. Abraham, *Armen* [1967] (Gouvernes: Le Tout sur le Tout, 1988), 13. A miraculous book. One of those that infallibly mark out a partition among readers between the worldly and the human. Need I say that I don't read much anymore, that everything just falls out of my hands? But Abraham's masterpiece held, held me. It was undoubtedly a factor in my sudden change of life. As if it wasn't so much that I reread *Armen*, but that it reread me, brought me back to myself.

22. When Brel said this (cited by Philippe Joubin, 'La cathédrale de Jacques Brel', *Voiles et Voiliers* 554 [April 2017], 113), he was in the Marquesas, at the end of a half round-the-world trip with a skeleton crew, on board the *Askøy II*, an eighteen-metre steel yawl weighing 42 tonnes, which was so poorly balanced that it couldn't be left under windvane

control or automatic pilot.... But it would be wrong to minimise the significance of the words.

23. M. Blanchot, *The Writing of the Disaster*, tr. A. Smock (Lincoln, NB and London: University of Nebraska Press), 122.

24. '*Tu es infâme. —Non, je suis une femme* [*You are awful. —No, I am a woman*]', as Jean-Claude Brialy and Anna Karina say in Godard's *Une femme est une femme* (1961). Not women [*les femmes*], the instance of infamy, but woman [*la femme*], who exists only in mothers. Woman, common woman, bears the world; women, rare as they are, suspend it. Hence I hate woman, that is to say mothers, even though I love women, and my mother.

25. See *Déclarer la gnose*, an 'ingenious' book (according to Guy Lardreau's endorsement) in which I cobbled together the preconditions for anti-philosophy out of a philosophy, or rather a reason at once generalised and disassembled into detached pieces.

26. G. Perros, *Papiers collés I* [1960] (Paris: Gallimard, 2019), 201.

27. A daily practice for since 2014 at least, photography has taken up the baton of speech, but not so as to speak 'that which cannot be said but only shown'; it is, in principle, a speaking of silence.

28. 'The sea bides its time,' recounts the celebrated lifeguard François Mic; 'lies in wait, like a crocodile; and swallows all. It is unforgiving. The sea doesn't like human beings. The sea is evil...God, it's evil!' (*Le Monde*, 19 July 1996, quoted by Björn Larsson in *From Cape Wrath to Finisterre: Sailing the Celtic Fringe* [London: Haus, 2012], 48). Jean-Pierre Abraham too, at the end of his life, confessed: 'I have seen old men drowned, and I have hated the sea ever since. And now I am constantly afraid.' (J.-P. Abraham, *Fort Cigogne* [Cognac: Le Temps qu'il fait, 1995]). '*Odi et amo* may well be the confession of those who consciously or blindly

have surrendered their existence to the fascination of the sea' (J. Conrad, 'The Mirror of the Sea', in *A Personal Record and The Mirror of the Sea* [London: Penguin, 1998], 249). Such is the confession of the sailor, who wavers 'ceaselessly and without any transition from love to hate' of the sea (L. Cozan, *Un feu sur la mer: Mémoires d'un gardien de phare* [Beignon: Les Oiseaux de Papier, 2010; second edition Ouessant: Les Îliennes, 2019], 122).

29. H. Queffélec, *Tempête sur Douarnenez* (Paris: Mercure de France, 1951), cited in P. Bazantay, *Tabarly* (Paris: François Bourin, 2019), 46–47.

30. Dir. Pierre Schoendoerffer, France, 1977.

31. 'The genuine gain with Fichte and Kant lies in the *method*—in the *regularization of genius*.' Novalis, *Notes for a Romantic Encyclopedia: Das Allgemeine Brouillon*, tr., ed. D.W. Wood (New York: SUNY Press, 2007), 164 [§921].

32. I refer here to Ray Brassier's *Nihil Unbound: Enlightenment and Extinction* (Basingstoke: Palgrave Macmillan, 2007). In spite of a close friendship with the author in the early 2000s (or perhaps because of it), it took me a long time to understand this book—that is to say, ultimately, to understand nihilism itself.

33. L. de Sutter, 'L'âge de l'anesthésie dont je parle est en réalité l'âge de la dépression', interview with J. Daudy and M. Perre, *Un philosophe*, <http://unphilosophe.com/2017/10/30/entretien-avec-laurent-de-sutter-lage-de-lanesthesie-dont-je-parle-est-en-realite-lage-de-la-depression/>.

34. 'The only human thing about humanity is what supplements its humanity—the innumerable accessories which, from language to fire, from books to computers, from tractors to cosmetics, make us what we are. Human ontology is a prosthetic ontology. Without prostheses, we

are just naked worms—neotenous larvae. The machine is our condition.' Laurent de Sutter, Facebook post, 20 September 2017.

35. J.-J. Rousseau, *The Social Contract and Other Later Political Writings*, ed. V. Gourevitch (Cambridge: Cambridge University Press, 1997), 54.

36. C. Jambet, *La Grande résurrection d'Alamût. Les formes de la liberté dans le shi'isme ismaélien* (Lagrasse: Verdier, 1990), 389.

37. Jean Epstein, cited by Pierre Salaün in *Île de Sein* (Rennes: Éditions Ouest-France, 1997), 30.

38. Louis Cozan, videoconference interview for the TV magazine show *Littoral*, 13 April 2020, <https://www.facebook.com/marinebarnerias.littoral/videos/2547347622248482>. To work in prisons, as I did at one time, precisely meant working to help prisoners escape from the imaginary half-baked idea of freedom that the lighthouse keeper denounces here.

39. 'Our world of fabricated products does not define itself as the sum of single, finalised pieces, but rather as a process: the daily new production of things which are daily new. The world of products does hence not "define" itself at all. It is indefinite, open, malleable, daily intent on reforming itself, daily adaptable to new situations [...].' G. Anders, 'Promethean Shame', in *Prometheanism: Technology, Digital Culture and Human Obsolescence*, ed C.J. Miller (London and New York: Rowman and Littlefield, 2016), 38.

40. F. Worms, 'L'ouverture, oui mais laquelle?', *Libération*, 7 April 2017.

41. In a visit to Brittany at the end of his mandate, President François Hollande declared: 'We need fresh air, because there are ill winds blowing [...], the winds of nationalism, of withdrawal into oneself, of fear. We must [...] move towards the open sea, and never withdraw' (as reported by Solenn de Royer, *Le Monde*, 29 April 2017).

42. M. Le Bris, *Un hiver en Bretagne* (Paris: NiL, 1996, republished Seuil, 1997), 189.

43. We know that the Brittany of the *Matter of Brittany*—a collection of legends and songs which, in the Middle Ages, gave rise to an immense literature—was not limited to what currently goes by that name, but encompassed also, and may even have centred on, the island of Britain. It matters little, regardless of the perceived necessity to distance Brittany from 'Celticity'.

44. Not that there was any conclusion to my research of the time. After taking my *khâgne* class, sailing at first from Concarneau, Vannes and Paimpol, I spent a great deal of time in Brittany, and seriously thought about *going back* to join the fight for its independence. That's not exactly a small thing. But on the one hand, I still believed in the state, and the mediocrity of activist minorities was repugnant to me,[b] while on the other hand, and above all, my despair of myself was greater than my hopes for Brittany: far from being the culmination of my quest at the time, it was an opportunity for me to have done with it—that is to say, to have done with myself (similarly, I later considered joining the Oratoire de France). So in the end, while thinking of concluding my research via recourse to an imaginary Brittany, I refused to draw from the real of Brittany any conclusions for my research.

(b) Thirty years later, when I have been back for ten years, the state is a zombie, and the activist minority little more than folklore. To see Breton militants making demands (for peanuts—the administrative reunification of the five Breton *départements*, or the preservation of the teaching of the Breton and Gallo languages in schools in Brittany, or reasonable accommodations such as democratisation by devolution promoted by Yann Lukas, the heir of Morvan Lebesque, or, along the same federalist lines, Frédéric Morvan and certain others) to a French state that is now essentially little more than a headless chicken still running around, is to weep with shame and anger. The image that springs to mind is not so much that of the child tugging at its mother's skirts to get a little attention, but that of the battered wife who, since it certainly isn't easy to separate from her brain-dead torturer, remains under his thumb, just letting out a little cry every now and again (the net effect of which is to remind France of precisely why it continues to mistreat Brittany, and why there is nothing to be ashamed about in doing so).

45. A. Le Cloarec, *Aux origines des mouvements bretons* (Spézet: Coop Breizh, 2016), 46.

46. I refer here to philosophy as a function, rather than as a discipline. A function of sufficient s(p)ecularisation, i.e. of encompassing and self-encompassing, of the mastery of masteries, almost always exercised not by itself under its own name, but by or through politics, religion, or economics, its three main placeholders, its *lieu-tenants*. From above the formation of the world, from below the adaptation of humans to the world, their transformation into worldly socialites, philosophy is a second-degree practice: the (transcendental) practice of (empirical) practices. Its place can be and in fact usually is taken by any first-degree practice, with that practice consequently hypostasised as s(p)ecular mastery. In the absence of an explicit philosophy, a placeholder occupies a place that cannot remain vacant. As the keystone of reality in its totalisation and self-aggregation, its world-making, the function of philosophy is absolutely necessary; on the other hand, what occupies its place is everything that is contingent. There is even every reason to consider that philosophy never performs its function better than when it does not act itself, openly, but is hidden, occulted, in so far as absence is its supreme mode of presence, in which it applies its customary disciplinary aspect to itself, like some cantankerous old lady left to the care of the university-hospice.

47. E. Cioran, *Cahiers, 1957–1972* (Paris: Gallimard, 1997), 128.

48. J. Michelet, *Histoire de France* (Paris: Lacroix, 19 vols., 1876), vol. 2, book 3, 'Tableau de France'.

49. So what is philosophy, envisaged now from a *disciplinary* point of view? That which is born of and eternalises itself by refusing and, to the full extent of the possible, as Aristotle says, by absorbing— vampirising— anti-philosophy. Plato having opened up both paths, that of the soul and that of the world, the path of the *Phaedo* and the *Republic* and the path of the *Timaeus* and the *Laws*, and Aristotle having, as we know, favoured the path of *the right* ('Aristotle was the preceptor of Alexander the Great, a corrupt of the first order, and what is more the inventor of academic philosophy!' as Badiou summarises [*Alain Badiou par Alain Badiou* (Paris: PUF, 2021), 65–66]).

50. See B.S. Paulsson, 'Radiocarbon Dates and Bayesian Modeling Support Maritime Diffusion Model for Megaliths in Europe', *Proceedings of the National Academy of Sciences of the United States of America* 116:9 (26 February 2019), 3460–65. This study suggests that Armorica was not one of the birthplaces but the one and only birthplace of megalithism in Europe, seven millennia ago, it having then been rapidly diffused without alteration, or in any case homogeneously, esentially via maritime routes. But in what way does this remarkable result help strengthen, or at least do no harm to, my suggestion regarding Brittany's radical preceding of the world?

An epistemological, or rather gnoseological point, first of all. As antiempiricist as my materialism may be, I do not reject the contribution of the empirical sciences; I simply *do not set out from them*. As summarised in theses IV ('Materialism brooks no compromise with any science that presents matter') and XII ('Materialism bases itself on all sciences, each of which presents matter') of Guy Lardreau's tract *Vive le matérialisme!* (Paris: Verdier, 2001), 9, 11, 18–19. A stance that requires that thought, *in order to think rather than merely prattle*, must moor itself to a positive discipline. This mooring must be of the order of an integral subjectivation, as sailing is for me. In other words, something very different from the imposture of a thinking 'hitched up' to the positivity of a discipline selected externally (examples of which are abundant).

Now, what I find in this case in the advances of archaeological science is a material amplification of my research. Not some kind of absurd empirical, chronological and anthropological 'confirmation' of the radical antecedence of Brittany to the world, as if the world could furnish a validation or 'proof' of the anti-worldly character of Brittany. But a coincidence *via superposition* of these precessions, which do not so much reflect one another as add to one another.

51. J.-P. Abraham, 'Rendez-vous à Ouessant' (1992), in *La Place royale* (Cognac: Le Temps qu'il fait, 2004), 79–80 (emphasis mine).

52. Saint-Pol-Roux, cited without precise references by Gérard Macé in 'L'œuvre en miettes de Saint-Pol-Roux', the introduction to his edition of the author's *Le Trésor de l'Homme* (Mortemart: Rougerie, 1991), 13.

53. Saint-Pol-Roux, 'Bretagne est univers', in *La Besace du solitaire*, 105.

54. The cardinal opposition between stasis and human enclosures and flux and worldly openings is present—structuring, even—in Barbara Stiegler's book *« Il faut s'adapter ». Sur un nouvel impératif politique* (Paris: Gallimard, 2018).

55. Breton reality is that of the reasonable, those who live in-between sentimentalism and business, and for whom there is one Brittany 'of legend and dream' and another 'of unavoidable realities', the somewhat sordid side, the latter looking to the former for a supplement of soul that is all the more precious in that it voluntarily offers itself up to commercialisation (since, beyond tourism alone, Brittany is a brand: 'Brittany' sells). And it is also that of the identitarians, who certainly struggle against the world, but only with the means of the world, *as if the flux of the world could furnish some stasis that would not be directly profitable to it.*

56. G. Perros, '*Papiers collés III*' [1978], in *Œuvres* (Paris: Gallimard, 2017), 1364.

57. A. Le Braz, *La Bretagne à travers l'Histoire* [1923] (Paris: Les Équateurs, 2009), 57. This brief late text by Le Braz, who died in 1926, is a
jewel whose erudition, intuition, and inspiration, in spite of being full of
a 'Celticity' typical of a certain era, rendered well and truly obsolete by
archaeological work of recent years,[c] go to make up one of the greatest
manifestos for Brittany.

(c) I refer here to the remarkable synthetic works of Yannick Lecerf (to
which I was introduced by his brief interview 'Qu'on se le dise: les Bretons
ne sont pas celtes', *La Nouvelle République*, 25 November 2014), namely
*La Bretagne préhistorique. Les peuplements, des origines à la conquête
romaine* (Morlaix: Skol Vreizh, 2014), and the indispensable *Bretons et
Celtes. Quand le monde de l'archéologie s'interroge ou les incertitudes
de la celtitude* (Le Coudray-Macouard: Feuillage éditions, 2017).

58. Perros, 'Bretagne', in *Papiers collés I*, 182.

59. For the distinction between the *as such* [*comme tel*] and the *as is*
[*tel quel*], I draw upon theorem 88 of François Laruelle's *A Biography of
Ordinary Man: Of Authorities and Minorities*, tr. J. Hock and A. Dubilet
(Cambridge: Polity, 2018), 151–52. Allow me to take advantage of this
technical reference to say how much I admire this incredible book, one
of the greatest of all time perhaps, a book which, moreover, is ultimately
considered by its author himself almost as the only one he wrote (see his
interview of 3 February 2021 with Narciso Aksayam, in *#Transistor* [DVD-
ROM] (Plancey-l'Abbaye: INgens, 2012), at 23'00''.

60. Saint-Pol-Roux, 'Carnets', in *Le Trésor de l'Homme*, 85.

61. Separated from the world by their mere existence, solitaries are at
this stage, in their doubled solitude, appropriated, threatened with going
no further, s(p)ecularising themselves. Identifying themselves with their
solitude, which is now weighed down with more sufficiency than any
social worldliness, they make their refusal of the world worldly by building
some inner citadel for themselves. This is the heart of Stoicism, 'the Stoic

plague' as Lardreau calls it,[d] a tradition which itself is the beating heart of all Western philosophy. 'This conception of the "I" [*moi*] as self-sufficient is one of the essential marks of the bourgeois spirit and its philosophy,' in the fine words of Emmanuel Levinas (many of whose analyses I share but almost all of whose positive propositions I reject). 'As sufficiency for the petty bourgeois, this conception of the "I" nevertheless nourishes the audacious dreams of a restless and enterprising capitalism. This conception presides over capitalism's work ethic, its cult of initiative and discovery, which aims less at reconciling man with himself than at securing for him the unknowns of time and things' (E. Levinas, *On Escape*, tr. B. Bergo [Stanford, CA: Stanford University Press, 2003], 68). Solitude left to its own devices, spontaneously s(p)ecularised, far from holding the world at a distance by means other than constant chatter, thus offers itself as the pivot of the most unbridled worldliness.

(d) G. Lardreau, *L'Exercice différé de la philosophie. À l'occasion de Deleuze* (Paris: Verdier, 1999), 51.

62. V. La Soudière, *Brisants*, ed. S. Massias (Orbey: Arfuyen, 2003), 91.

63. A pre-publication version of the Canon, entitled 'Prolégomènes à la Bretagne. Anti-politique du navigateur solitaire', appeared in the journal *Filozofski vestnik*, 39: 2 (2018). This pre-publication, and the editorial support that made it possible in the tactful and generous person of Jason Barker, played an important role in the development of the present work, of which that text was a first crystallisation.

64. According to Slavoj Žižek, illuminating—and illuminated by—Hegelian logic, in *Less Than Nothing: Hegel and the Shadow of Dialectical Materialism* (London and New York: Verso, 2012), 276–77.

65. Rather than taking a dialectical rather than a materialist turn and holding that the subject is only ever a subjectivised predicate (as Žižek does in *Less than Nothing*, 529–36) or following a turn more spiritualist than transcendental and trying to trace back from the predicate to

its subjective conditions of possibility, it is a question of considering the predicate as the occasion, not the correlate, of a subjectivation that itself is ante-predicative.

66. J. Gracq, 'Lettrines 2' [1974], in Œuvres complètes (Paris: Gallimard, 2 vols, 1995), vol. 2, 271.

67. Le Braz, La Bretagne à travers l'Histoire, 84–85. I would be willing to draw a parallel here, mutatis mutandis, between megalithism and Christianity. 'Christianity, which seems to participate in the cultural revolution, and indeed does in certain respects participate in it, was ultimately constructed as a cultural counter-revolution; it ended up becoming the ideological revolution itself, the most assured counterattack against the cultural revolution. In it we find all the themes of the cultural revolution, but domesticated', writes Guy Lardreau in L'Ange (in collaboration with Christian Jambet [Paris: Grasset, 1976], 99). In the same way, megalithism, as an Armorican invention (see note 50), would be an escape from socialisation and the bonds of servitude that make up the world, to the point of turning the angelic can(n)on into an instrument for closing off the booming Neolithic world from above: from a gnosis to a commodified supplement of soul.

68. Whether or not it belongs to the impasse of the cultural revolution, the power of the civilisational development of Armorican megalithism is not in question here. It is in this direction that, following archaeologist Yannick Lecerf (cf. sub-note (c) above), we must look for the key to understanding the cultural, linguistic, and even anthropological stabilities erroneously attributed to Celticity. Not only did the Celts not settle in Brittany, since as a migrant people they were not interested in the peninsulas, but, as they sought to blend in with the populations, they failed 'to integrate themselves into Breton communities because of the strong identity they had developed in the Neolithic period' ('Let it be known: the Bretons are not Celts'). Nonetheless, they could very well have occupied the south-east of England, ignoring the rest of the British Isles

(Lecerf, *Bretons et Celtes*, 149–59). In short, prepared to play the game of appeasement at the terminological level, Lecerf considers it viable to continue to describe as 'Celtic' phenomena 'whose origin lies in ancient prehistorical sources' and 'linguistic proximities whose origin on the Atlantic seaboard appears to predate by several millennia the reference migrations', but only as long as 'all confusion with the migratory movements recognised during the Iron Age in central Europe is avoided' (ibid, 168–69). I have no such scruples, as the register of the 'Celtic', employed for identitarian purposes ad nauseum, does little to help us think. The important thing for me is to establish the extreme depth of the imprint of a primordial Armorican civilisation which, to use Le Braz's words while shifting their point of application, is in contact with 'the granite, the indestructible rock upon which the Breton soul rests and to which it owes its having remained, consistent even in its inconsistencies, indefectibly identical to itself' (*La Bretagne à travers l'Histoire*, 82). If it were confirmed that European megalithism was invented there, rather than in the misty North, the steppes of Eurasia, or the Mediterranean basin, where it spread with a 'similarity of construction techniques, and notable similarities as much in the choice of location as in the plans or elevations found there [which] cannot be the result of simple coincidences', this would turn Brittany's anti-worldliness into the keystone of the world; it would place Brittany at the heart of a primordial Europe, an 'open world linked by the sea' where 'the strong cultural identity still very present among certain peoples today in search of their origins' (to quote Lecerf, ibid., 19–20) was born.

69. *Henge*: A prehistoric circular structure forming a sort of enclosure. *Vit* [member, penis], from the Latin *vectio*, bar, lever. Which is what the Breton peninsula is qua can(n)on of circumscription, qua can(n)on that constitutes its circumscription.

70. E. d'Ors, *Du baroque* [1935], tr. A. Rouart-Valéry (Paris: Gallimard, 2000), cited by Kenneth White in *Les Finisterres de l'esprit. Rimbaud, Segalen et moi-même* [1998] (Paris: Isolato, new edition, 2007), 53.

I allow myself a rancorous word here against White's book, whose sub-lime title, and whose protagonists, each in various impassioning ways, led me to hope for marvels, whereas what I find in it is nothing but an all too dispensable series of disjointed platitudes.[e] Apart from Pascal Quignard's *Sur l'idée d'une communauté de solitaires* (Paris: Arléa, 2015), which inspires the same kind of spite in me, I don't remember ever having been quite so disappointed by a book whose title, in itself and in relation to its author's other works, inspired such high hopes. *Never mess with titles*.

(e) Far be it from me to blame Kenneth White for the disjointed charac-ter of his text in its materiality—that would be a failure on my part, when I myself can say, with Rousseau, 'I throw my scattered and incomplete thoughts down on rags of paper, and then I sew it all together as best I can, and that's how I write a book. And see what a book it is! I enjoy meditating, researching, inventing, what disgusts me is putting things in order; and the proof that I have less reasoning than I have wit is that the transitions are always what cost me the most: this would not be the case were the ideas all seamlessly connected in my head' (J.-J. Rousseau, 'Mon portrait', in *Œuvres complètes* [Paris: Pléiade, 5 volumes, 1959–95], vol. 1, 1120–29). No, what I believe I can farily charge him with is having camouflaged beneath a discourse that is seamlessly connected, not to mention fuelled by magnificent borrowings, an enterprise that is actually entirely disjointed, rough around the edges—adrift, to use an expression he is fond of—and with having delayed again and again, until it is too late, the moment to treat the notion of finisterre no longer as a vague metaphor but for and in itself, in line with what he himself sets out in as many words as being the object of his book: 'to approach the confines of the world and describe a situation at the limits, it being understood that "limit" means not only the place where something ends, but also the place where something begins' (ibid., 54). Bergson and Lardreau had little in common other than the probity of considering that one is never obliged to write a book, and that there is only a book when it is constrained by that which it brings together.

71. V. Segalen, letter to Henri Manceron, 23 September 1911, cited in White, *Les finisterres de l'esprit*, 19.

72. By a surprising chance, I once met Michel Le Bris on the street in Morlaix. It was in 2009, when I was on a forced stopover in Roscoff for a few weeks after breaking two fingers of one hand during a manoeuvre. As I had just started to read some of his texts, including *Un hiver en Bretagne*, I was wondering as I walked along whether it might be possible to try and meet with him if he was around at the time. I looked up and, just as Captain Haddock at the beginning of *The Red Sea Sharks* mentions General Alcazar only to bump into him the very next moment, I recognised Le Bris passing by. At first stunned, then doubting what had just happened, I continued along my way, in the opposite direction to him. Later that day, no longer thinking about it, I went into a chandlery in the port. There was Le Bris, buying parts to repair the mooring of his dinghy, which had run aground. I took my courage in both hands and went to say hello, to make contact; but, shy as I can be, and worldly as his angelic downfall had led him to satisfy himself with being—as is the case also with Christian Jambet, Olivier Rolin, Jean-Pierre Le Dantec…Guy Lardreau, in all his devastated rigour, being the exception to the rule—the encounter did not take place.

Beyond the mere anecdote, for me this point is essential. In it is condensed all the ambiguity of the legacy extorted from these masters I chose for myself. Extorted rather than received, for they are masters who give nothing. Echoing my own experience, Jean Birnbaum severely reproaches them: 'Those hosts offer neither attention nor any particular kindness. Ultimately, they have little to give you, not even a bibliographical reference: they have read everything but cite no one, especially living authors. You will never be their pupil, though you will perhaps have the chance to become their servant. If the ['68] Generation has no pedagogical desire, it is moved by a violent drive to mastery' (J. Birnbaum, *Les Maoccidents. Un néoconservatisme à la française* [Paris: Stock, 2009], 20). For my part, I have no such reproaches to make. Transmission or lack thereof is the least of my worries. Only one thing matters to me:

if I am a subject, then I owe it to those masters. They gave nothing but that, which is a subtraction, and is priceless. Yet I am infinitely angry with them, as they are probably angry with themselves, for having converted their once intransigent angelism into complacent worldliness. I resent them as much as they resent not having flown away, still being stuck in the world.

For my masters were archangels. 'I think of a phrase of [Robert Louis] Stevenson's', says Le Bris in his interviews with Yvon Le Men. 'He found himself at Menton, sick, desperate, at the age of twenty-three, and we might say that he could no longer hold onto life. And he writes to his friend Fanny Sitwell: "To sit by the sea and to be conscious of nothing but the sound of the waves, and the sunshine over all your body, is not unpleasant; but I was an Archangel once." *Well! I myself was an archangel once.'* (M. Le Bris, *Fragments du royaume* [Genouilleux: La Passe du Vent, 2000], 55, emphasis mine.) But how ugly fallen archangels are! However great they may be in the eyes of their contemporaries, their worldly enjoyment of the abjection of knowledge and power, a certain form of power, makes their angelic decay something very dirty. 'He was pure. In contact with the world, that makes for someone extremely dirty', writes Tristan Garcia (*Hate: A Romance*, tr. M. Duvert and L. Stein [London: Faber, 2012], 303). As described by Pavese before him: 'It is dangerous to be too angelic: when the world treats you as it has always (and legitimately) treated angels, with cruelty or off-hand amusement, you at once become the worst and most depraved of demons. One, for instance, who, incapable of doing harm, takes a whole day to kill a rabbit, because every now and then he stops to reproach himself, and doesn't go on until he convinces himself that the whimpering rabbit is making a fuss about nothing. *Nothing is more warped than a fallen angel.'* (*This Business of Living*, 91 [7 June 1938], emphasis mine).

73. K. White, *En toute candeur*, tr. P. Leyris (Paris: Mercure de France, 1964), 63.

74. K. White, *Le Lieu et la Parole. Entretiens 1987–1997* (Cléguer: Éditions du Scorff, 1997), 13, 11.

75. 'Saint-Pol-Roux, that southerner who had taken up residence in Brittany, as a granite place of resistance', writes Kenneth White (*Les Finisterres de l'esprit*, 20). And elsewhere, this time speaking of himself: 'Brittany is enough for me, more than enough, even. In it I find a space that suits me, and in this space I think more and more in terms of resistance and insularity. Resistance to mediocratisation [...], a resistance that is all laughter (like a laughing seagull), research, and creation. As far as insularity is concerned, strategically speaking, now I envision only islands, islets—possibly forming an archipelago' ('Une stratégie du passage ou l'Épître des sept îles', *Europe* 913 [May 2005], 143).

76. White, *Le Lieu et la Parole*, 50.

77. White, 'Une stratégie du passage', 143–44.

78. White, *Le Lieu et la Parole*, 109.

79. A dispute in which Deleuze, who in 1979 was a member of the jury for White's PhD thesis (where he voiced the appropriate admiration befitting such occasions, often more worldly than subjectivated), endeavours to disqualify the candidate by reducing his celticism to some racialist temptation, so as to trigger against him, among the cultivated public and everything that counts in terms of the mediation of thought, the reflex of the *cordon sanitaire* (a cordon whose truth is obviously constrictive). See G. Deleuze and F. Guattari, *A Thousand Plateaus*, tr. B. Massumi (Minneapolis: University of Minnesota Press, 1987), 379, and K. White, *Dialogue avec Deleuze. Politique, philosophie, géopoétique* (Paris: Isolato, 2007).

80. Deleuze and Guattari, *A Thousand Plateaus*, 381.

81. 'A ship is a beauty and a mystery wherever we see it', observes Harriet Beecher-Stowe (*The Pearl of Orr's Island: A Story of the Coast of Maine* [1862] [Project Gutenberg eBook], chapter 30, 291).

82. S. Valdinoci, *L'Europanalyse et les structures d'une autre vie. Le feu de la pensée sacrée* (Paris: L'Harmattan, 2001), 7 [emphasis mine]. I am far from having taken the full measure of this fascinating book, which I consider a masterpiece, and in which complete illegibility alternates with a profound (and at moments limpid) critical erudition and absolutely astonishing searing flashes, the whole in an atmosphere of grace of which I know few examples. (I am not so dazzled by the author's writing in general, which is often laborious; but the lack of recognition for his work is scandalous.)

83. My boat is not particularly fast, most of the time around 5 knots. Although she has sometimes reached remarkable speeds, this remains an exception. In May 2015, for example, she was clocked at 15.7 knots GPS between Brittany and the Azores. According to the Grib files, the wind speed was 35 knots from the east, probably 40 knots on the water. Faster still, it was at 17.2 knots GPS that Jean-Michel Sautter's crew set off in 2004 in the long swell of the Atlantic, returning from the West Indies at the end of her great round-the-world voyage. At the time, the wind speed was 45 knots. In both cases, the boat was on automatic pilot with no one outside. I was asleep; Sautter and his crew were playing cards.

This is an opportunity to say a little more about my *Theorème*, the Globe-flotteur 33 thanks to which I manage to traverse this life for which I am not made. Among her outstanding characteristics there is, as you will have understood, a great directional stability, which she owes to her two drop keels: the pivoting centreboard (for a draught of 0.9 metres in the upper position and 2.25 metres in the lower position), and the rear daggerboard which when sailing downwind keeps her on a straight track and when sailing close-hauled in a breeze makes the helm smooth, allowing her to be entrusted for days on end to the care of a small automatic pilot, without causing any excessive fatigue to the equipment, and with moderate power consumption. Another characteristic of the boat is her high passive safety. The shape of the hull and the volume of the roof give her a behaviour in heavy seas that is similar to that of a lifeboat. In addition to this, there is the remarkable, almost perfect protection of two major fragile elements of a boat, namely the leg of the sail-drive and, even more so, the rudder, and the extreme robustness of the construction: the thickness of the aluminium (12 millimetres for the vertical plating, 14 for the bilge, 20 at least, 24 perhaps, for the bottom of the hull) is already a guarantee of resistance to impacts of all kinds, but it also ensures great overall solidity thanks to the quality of the welds, made at very high current intensity, something that is not possible with conventional sheet metal thicknesses. Apart from its many qualities, not least its low sensitivity to corrosion, Strongall® has two drawbacks: the weight, which is less than that of steel but greater than that of a conventional aluminium construction, and the aesthetics of the edges, which are cut to size. Although I really like the hull of my boat, her deck plan, and her general appearance when viewed from a three-quarter angle, her profile, all ridges, bulky even when the hull is quite low on the water, is not so pleasant to look at. Sometimes I think the two of us have the same problem there.

84. J.-F. Deniau, *La Mer est ronde* [1981] (Paris: Gallimard, 1992), 253–54. This great pleasure sailor and fine writer was above all a socialite, in the most complete sense of the word one can imagine (a grand bourgeois, diplomat, parliamentarian, minister, European commissioner, *académicien*...). Everything he has to say relates to the world, or to a world—including what he says about the sea. Nonetheless, read very early and often reread since, this book, like those of Jean-Michel Barrault, has helped me explain to myself what it is that has always attracted me so strongly to boats.

85. I remember the dyspeptic reactions of leading nautical journalists who could not forgive Titouan Lamazou for the biting lucidity of certain statements that his victory in the inaugural Vendée Globe made it impossible

for them to ignore. They judged him haughty and sinister, scandalously out of tune with the fun, smiling, dreamy imagery of sailing that helps the nautical business and its sponsors to grow and the specialised press to sell pages of advertising. What did Lamazou say that was so shocking? He merely pointed out the strictly worldly nature of sailing: 'I like to think that we professional sailors deserve to be recognised as part of the history of "working sailors". As far back as I can remember, it seems to me that no boat was ever designed or built for the sole purpose of sailing. It is a delusion of our times to think that going to sea, in itself, can bring any happiness. We receive blow upon blow, the waves crash into our faces. There are endless annoyances, not to mention the Kafkaesque alienation involved in perpetually maintaining these floating machines. Even if the sea is only a way for us to get our share of glory, it remains a job. When the tall ships left India carrying their cargo of tea, they would race to get to London first in order to sell their cargo at the peak of demand. In the same way, we peddle the image of our shipowners, now called sponsors, and this time I too have brought my cargo of Écureuil and Aquitaine to safe harbour' ('Voici ma cargaison d'Écureuil et d'Aquitaine', *Neptune Yachting* 71 [May 1990], 77).

86. This formula, which I thought I had come up with myself, is in fact Gilles Lapouge's, just as he has a version of the opposition between radical and worldly boats, that of pirate ships and merchant ships: 'When [the pirate] prowls the ocean, it is not with a view to reducing or eliminating the space between two continents or cities. On the contrary, his purpose is to constantly broaden this space, to maintain the gap, to make the water prevail over the land [...]. By pursuing merchant ships, he unravels the network that society weaves upon the sea,' he writes in *Les Pirates. Forbans, flibustiers, boucaniers et autres gueux de mer* [1969] (Paris: Phébus, 2006) (161), a brilliant book that I have read so many times that it has obviously become imprinted on me.

87. A book, a true book in any case—one that owes less to what it says than to the void around which it is written, which swallows it up at the same time it engenders it—is a kind of finisterre.

88. X. Grall, 'La mer restituée...', *Le Monde*, 26 September 1977, reprinted in *Et parlez-moi de la terre...* (Dinan: Terre de Brume, 2013), 54.

89. Abraham, *Armen*, 59–60.

90. 'The Armen', not Armen or the Armen lighthouse. This is what the inhabitants of the Île de Sein themselves call it according to Louis Cozan, keeper, not of the Armen, but of the Île de Sein lighthouse (having also spent time at la Jument, Kéréon, le Stiff, le Créac'h and les Pierres Noires, before his return to Kéréon) (Cozan, *Un feu sur la mer*, 75).

91. Jean-Pierre Abraham, in 'Ar'men', report by Jean Pradinas for the TV show *Les coulisses de l'exploit*, 19 December 1962, online on the INA site, <https://www.ina.fr/ina-eclaire-actu/video/cpf04007046/ar-men>, from 4'39''.

92. Vincent La Soudière, letter 152, Montégut, 26 August 1971, quoted on the Facebook page under his name on 5 April 2017. Not for lack of searching, on many trips, to Spain and Denmark in particular, and during sojourns at the abbey of Notre-Dame de Belloc in the Basque country, and at Lérins Abbey, where the finisterre of the monastery doubles that of the island. With no place for himself, with nothing to defend himself from the world, no wonder he ended up drawing the conclusion, in a 1974 letter, that he was 'not fit to exist'. No one, without a place, and without the organon that one can forge for oneself in a place, is fit to exist. Consequently, only two solutions were available to him: either to become worldly, following the example, perhaps, of Cioran, to whom he was quite close; or to commit suicide. Consistent to the end, La Soudière killed himself in the very heart of the world: in Paris, by throwing himself into the Seine.

93. Difficult not to cite this fragment here: 'Sad sailor, in the depths of your sickroom, you know well that no voyage will any longer be granted to you, and between your feverish fingers you clutch those little paper ships that punctuate your futile hours and which will never set sail.' (La Soudière, *Brisants*, 23).

94. See É. Tabarly, *Mémoires du large* [1997] (Paris: Le Livre de Poche, 1998), and Conrad, *The Mirror of the Sea*: 'Of all the living creatures upon land and sea, it is ships alone that cannot be taken in by barren pretences [...]'. If sailing, whether radical or not, is an activity that does not suit impostors, 'Navigation 2.0', on the contrary, has seen them proliferate. And for good reason: doesn't it describe itself as a form of surfing?

95. La Soudière, *Brisants*, 32.

96. In spite of their legendary attachment to Brittany, 'many are the Bretons who have embarked as state sailors or navymen on long voyages around the world. But what they love is the sea—that is to say, the element which, to their eyes, is still Breton.' (A. Loyen, 'L'âme bretonne', in *Annales de Bretagne* 54:1 [1947], 24n2.)

97. Contrary to what I used to think, drowning at sea is probably not such a terrible death—perhaps it is even a rather sweet way to die, as suggested in the account of the single-handed sailor Florence Arthaud, who fell into the water off Cape Corsica on 29 October 2011 while crouching over the stern of her boat to relieve herself: 'I'm losing strength. I begin to swallow an alarming amount of water. I try to reassure myself. I tell myself that it's not so bad, that it will clean me out, give me a little enema. Little by little I lose awareness of things, of the danger, of my loneliness and of death lurking. My reality evaporates and only appears to me in occasional flashes. I can feel the water coming in through my nose. I tell myself that this is not so bad either. But it goes straight into my lungs, I know that very well. In fact, I'm starting to become delirious. I have always been told that death by drowning is a pleasant death, without much suffering.

I have also been told that swallowing water through your nose is the beginning of the end. That at a certain point you are overtaken by the intoxication of the deep. You fall asleep, you are carried away, and you die without suffering.' F. Arthaud, with J.-L. Bachelet, *Cette nuit, la mer est noire* (Paris: Flammarion, 2016), 141–42.

98. G. Bachelard, *Water and Dreams: An Essay on the Imagination of Matter*, tr. E.R. Farrell (Dallas: Pegasus Foundation, 1983). '[D]eath associated with water is more dream-like than death associated with earth: the pain of water is infinite' (ibid., 6).

99. J. Lacan, 'Death is in the Domain of Faith' (conference paper in Louvain, 13 October 1972), tr. A. Chadwick, <http://www.lacanianworks.net/?p=12522>, 7 [translation modified].

100. Perros, 'Papiers collés I', *in Œuvres,* 417.

101a. Often attributed to Plato or Aristotle—I have no idea why—this statement seems to be a phrase of Anacharsis's, probably without any other significance than to emphasise the extent to which sailing is a perilous affair, the sailor never being separated from death by more than the thin membrane of a boat's hull.

101b. This theorem is the climax of Tract(atus) 23, a kind of 'text zero' of Theorrorism II, published and exhibited as a poster in a project by the artist Juan Pérez Agirregoikoa (*Concert pour poing levé* [Montreuil: Éditions Matière, 2007]), translated into English, Spanish, Dutch and Serbian, and reprinted in R. Mackay (ed.), *Collapse 6: Geophilosophy* (Falmouth: Urbanomic, 2010) and in *Identities* 15:1–2 (2018).

102. G.-A. Goldschmidt, *Jean-Jacques Rousseau ou l'esprit de solitude* (Paris: Phébus, 1978), 104.

103. Y. Le Corre, *L'Ivre de mer* (Tréguier, 2010), 28. A book that pushes its demand for coherence to the limit, having been printed with movable type on a hand press by the author himself, who says that learning typography 'was like learning another way to sail'.

104. Abraham, *Armen*, 135.

105. M. Riboulet, *Le Corps des anges* (Paris: Gallimard, 2005), 63–64.

106. *Theorrorism I* has a respect for jouissance, as opposed to the disgustingness of happiness. *Theorrorism II* marks out a jouissance untouched by happiness. Happiness does not exist, unlike the category of happiness, which does indeed exist all the more in so far as it is empty of content. Happiness is the central category of philosophy in general, not just its practical side, since it is the category under the auspices of whose void the great vocation of fabricating the world functions. The category of happiness exists, happiness does not. It is for tourists. And for those who 'take them for a (boat) ride' in search of wisdom. There is no happiness, only the cycle of pleasure and sorrow, amid the expanse of immense melancholy. Except that there is joy, there are rushes of joy, each of which is a traversal of melancholy.

107. Saint-John Perse, *Seamarks* [*Amers*, 1957], tr. W. Fowley (New York: Harper, 1958), 183; reprinted in *Collected Poems* (Princeton, NJ: Princeton University Press, 1983), 527.

108. B. Moitessier, *La Longue Route. Seul entre mers et ciels* [1971] (Paris: J'ai lu, 1994), 19.

109. E. Rousset, *L'Idéal chaviré* (Lagrasse: Verdier, 2000), 91. The sentence immediately preceding this one is worth quoting (as are many others in this stunning, meteoric book): 'Consciousness was not given to man as the beginning of knowledge, but for the obstruction of truth, for the parousia of Semblance.'

110. Abraham, *Armen*, 85, 135. 'But if you have a goal, the hours must comply with it,' he was once told. 'Not at all. They lead me', he replies (118). The sea sails, and the hours lead us.

111. G. Perros, *Poèmes bleus* [1962] (Paris: Gallimard, 2019), 58.

112. Conrad, 'The Mirror of the Sea', 140.

113. The great benefit of washing, cleaning, and tidying up is that setting things in order around oneself tempers the disorder within.

114. Twitter was the place and the instrument of my initial trials and tribulations along the path of a functional speech that comes from silence and leads back to it. And if my working toward the dispossessed sovereignty of a speech of silence proceeded in this way, it is because to tweet is already, by the very nature of its apparatus,[f] an *accomplished writing of melancholy*. Particularly when the use of Twitter takes on a ritualistic dimension. With, in my case, a twofold daily register: the writing of light and the writing of form, a photographic and theoretical framing of my life from day to day. (The essential being not so much exchanges—I've never considered Twitter to be a 'social network'; if I enter into exchanges on the platform, it is as an extra, a supplement—but publication, because to publish is to be able to read oneself: without the objectification of publication, there can be no real reading of one's own words; Twitter having the advantage that you can delete your own publications, which thus do not remain present as a permanent living rebuke.)

(f) In its apparatus, if not in the uses made of it, Twitter is not just a 'social network': in a certain sense it can even be said to prefigure the anti-social institution of a community of solitudes. It is already an institution, a screen separating and protecting me from the imaginary flood of the world by relating me to it in a symbolic mode: enough to support a daily trajectory of subjectivation, enough to stand up to the world a little each day. To force the issue: if Twitter is the vehicle of the I in the digital world, of a traversal of the self, Facebook is the capital of the self, the matrix of its endless inflation. If Twitter, as tool of subjectivation, can or could in some cases allow for the erasure of worldliness and the traversal of identities, Facebook, as a tool of unbridled socialisation, is the world itself and its tidal factory of identities. If Twitter is the accomplished writing of melancholy, Facebook is the writing of boredom.

115. E. Ionesco, *The Hermit*, tr. R. Seaver (London: Calder, 1983), 156.

116. E. Cioran, *Divagations* [1945], tr. N. Cavaillès (Paris: Gallimard, 2019), 26. This is Cioran's last text in Romanian, after which he wrote only in French. A text between two languages, then, like a lock in a canal—a position which undoubtedly contributes to its extreme acuity.

117. Whether calculation or dream, whether imaginary understanding or imagination, reflection is that with which we comfort ourselves. To reflect is to pretend to think in order not to think.

118. In which sense the man of ritual is neither a man of letters nor an intellectual: 'To perceive that life is more important than thought, means being a learned man, an intellectual; it means that his own thought has not become life.' Pavese, *This Business of Living*, 217.

119. C. Madézo, *Portuaires* (Rennes: La Part Commune, 2008), 76.

120. Conrad, 'The Mirror of the Sea', 242.

121. H. Melville, *Moby Dick* [1851] (Project Gutenberg eBook). Soulless as they may be, the promoters of management, and already those of the notion of 'employment', know very well that they are knee-deep in shit. Since not all the desks in the world have complete bastards sitting at them, many of these, metaphysicians in spite of themselves, having vomited up their souls, allow themselves a supplement: they have dreams. In many cases, they even dream of the sea.

122. This is particularly true in art, science, and sport. (Witness, among a thousand others, the brilliant ocean racer who, in a long retrospective interview on his career, does not even pretend to believe in an absolute. For him nothing exists but the quest for success, intensified by the fact that those around him, his childhood friends in particular, have achieved successes that he himself hasn't). In the same way, the overwhelming majority of books, and even more so academic articles, are written only to occupy the field, to hold one's own in research, as Althusser used to say, and to counter jealous colleagues by giving oneself the nobler pretexts of emulation and attention to the conjuncture.

123. A. Deneault, *Politiques de l'extrême centre* (Montréal: Lux, 2016), 93.

124. Since the world holds that radicalisation is a subjective figure of evil, all subjectivation in that world has *explicitly* become, by retroaction of the world, a figure of evil.

125. For example, I set up and ran a radicalisation workshop in prison for six months, within the framework of and with funding from the struggle against radicalisation in prisons.

126. The reference here is not to the Wittgenstein of the *Tractatus* (6.521) or he of the remarks collected in *Culture and Value*, but to Björn Larsson's reprise (in *From Cape Wrath to Finisterre*, 14–15), where he blithely adulterates Wittgenstein's vital singular (the problem of life) with a tourist plural (the problems of existence).

127. S. Weil, *Gravity and Grace*, tr. E. Crawford and M. von der Ruhr (London and New York: Routledge, 2002), 4.

128. J. Starobinski, 'Démocrite parle. L'utopie mélancolique de Robert Burton', *Le Débat* 29 (March 1984), 54–55.

129. Twitter, I insist, is great because of its smallness, its finite framework as an apparatus for circumscribing speech, one which conditions a relationship to the infinite. A device that curbs the easy complications of chatter by aiming at the difficult simplicity of the formula. What cannot be said in the (at first 140, then) 280 characters of a tweet rarely deserves to be said.

130. '[O]ne can recognise the very characteristic imprint of this Breton poetics in the use of a concise language, almost lapidary in the mineral sense of the word.' S. Gondolle, 'Le récit maritime breton', in S. Gondolle (ed.), *Bretagne et mer en écritures* (Rennes: PUR, 2008), 18. To give my formulae something to ricochet off, like pebbles thrown at full speed, to make my writing lapidary by any means available, including those of a *mineral* arrangement on the page. For 'the stone accepts the encirclement of silence [*tegemer ar maen kelc'hiadur an didrouz*]' (M.-J. Christien, *Pierre après pierre*, translated into Breton by C. Sauvaget [Quimperlé: Les Chemins Bleus, 2008], 18).

131. Biography turns life into writing, counter-biography turns writing into life ('Writing does not recount what has been lived, it precedes life' [A. Veinstein, on *Une vie de Roger Laporte*, in *Radio sauvage* (Paris: Seuil, 2010), 89]). As in Rousseau, anti-biography, the real beating heart of anti-philosophy, is the enunciation of a human solitude.

BIBLIOGRAPHY

Abraham, Jean-Pierre. *Armen*. Gouvernes: Le Tout sur le Tout, 1988.

——— *Fort-Cigogne*. Cognac: Le Temps qu'il fait, 1995.

——— *La Place royale*. Cognac: Le Temps qu'il fait, 2004.

Agirregoikoa, Juan Pérez. *Concert pour poing levé*. Montreuil: Éditions Matière, 2007.

Anders, Günther. 'Promethean Shame', in *Prometheanism: Technology, Digital Culture and Human Obsolescence*, ed C.J. Miller. London and New York: Rowman and Littlefield, 2016.

Antoine [Pierre Antoine Muraccioli]. *Voyage aux Amériques*. Paris: Arthaud, 1986.

——— *Mettre les voiles*. Paris: Arthaud, 2010.

Arthaud, Florence, with Jean-Louis Bachelet. *Cette nuit, la mer est noire*. Paris: Flammarion, 2016.

Bachelard, Gaston. *Water and Dreams: An Essay on the Imagination of Matter*, tr. E.R. Farrell. Dallas: Pegasus Foundation, 1983.

Badiou, Alain. *Alain Badiou par Alain Badiou*. Paris: PUF, 2021.

Bazantay, Pierre. *Tabarly*. Paris: François Bourin, 2019.

Beecher-Stowe, Harriet. *The Pearl of Orr's Island: A Story of the Coast of Maine*. Project Gutenberg eBook.

Birnbaum, Jean. *Les Maoccidents. Un néoconservatisme à la française*. Paris: Stock, 2009.

Blanchot, Maurice. *The Writing of the Disaster*, tr. A. Smock. Lincoln, NB and London: University of Nebraska Press.

Brassier, Ray. *Nihil Unbound: Enlightenment and Extinction*. Basingstoke: Palgrave Macmillan, 2007.

Christien, Marie-Josée. *Pierre après pierre*, tr. Claire Sauvaget. Quimperlé: Les Chemins Bleus, 2008.

Cioran, Emil. *Divagations*, tr. N. Cavaillès. Paris: Gallimard, 2019.

——— *Cahiers. 1957–1972*. Paris: Gallimard, 1997.

Conrad, Joseph. *A Personal Record and The Mirror of the Sea*. London: Penguin, 1998.

Cozan, Louis. *Un feu sur la mer: Mémoires d'un gardien de phare*. Ouessant: Les Îliennes, 2019.

D'Ors, Eugenio. *Du baroque*, tr. A. Rouart-Valéry. Paris: Gallimard, 2000.

BIBLIOGRAPHY

de Sutter, Laurent. 'L'âge de l'anesthésie dont je parle est en réalité l'âge de la dépression', *Un philosophe*, <http://unphilosophe. com/2017/10/ 30/entretien-avec-laurent-de-sutter-lage-de-lanesthesie-dont-je-parle-est-en-realite-lage-de-la-depression/>.

Deleuze, Gilles, and Félix Guattari. *A Thousand Plateaus*, tr. B. Massumi. Minneapolis: University of Minnesota Press, 1987.

Deneault, Alain. *Politiques de l'extrême centre*. Montréal: Lux, 2016.

Deniau, Jean-François. *La Mer est ronde*. Paris: Gallimard, 1992.

Elléouët, Yves. *Falc'hun*. Paris: Gallimard, 1976.

Garcia, Tristan. *Hate: A Romance*, tr. M. Duvert and L. Stein. London: Faber, 2012.

Goldschmidt, Georges-Arthur. *Jean-Jacques Rousseau ou l'esprit de solitude*. Paris: Phébus, 1978.

Gondolle, Sophie. 'Le récit maritime breton', in S. Gondolle (ed.), *Bretagne et mer en écritures*. Rennes: PUR, 2008.

Gracq, Julien. *Œuvres complètes*. Paris: Gallimard, 1995.

Grall, Xavier. *Et parlez-moi de la terre…*. Dinan: Terre de Brume, 2013

Grelet, Gilles. *Déclarer la gnose. D'une guerre qui revient à la culture*. Paris: L'Harmattan, 2002.

——— 'Theory is Waiting', in R. Mackay (ed.), *Collapse VI: Geo/Philosophy,* 477–83. Falmouth: Urbanomic, 2010.

——— 'Prolégomènes à la Bretagne. Anti-politique du navigateur solitaire'. *Filozofski vestnik*, 39: 2 (2018).

Ionesco, Eugène. *The Hermit*, tr. R. Seaver. London: Calder, 1983.

Jambet, Christian. *La Grande résurrection d'Alamût. Les formes de la liberté dans le shi'isme ismaélien*. Lagrasse: Verdier, 1990.

Joubin, Philippe. 'La cathédrale de Jacques Brel'. *Voiles et Voiliers* 554 (April 2017).

La Soudière, Vincent. *Brisants*, ed. S. Massias. Orbey: Arfuyen, 2003.

Lamazou, Titouan. 'Voici ma cargaison d'Écureuil et d'Aquitaine'. *Neptune Yachting* 71 (May 1990).

Lapouge, Gilles. *Les Pirates. Forbans, flibustiers, boucaniers et autres gueux de mer*. Paris: Phébus, 2006.

Lardreau, Guy. *La Mort de Joseph Staline. Bouffonnerie philosophique.* Paris: Grasset, 1978.

——— *L'Exercice différé de la philosophie. À l'occasion de Deleuze.* Paris: Verdier, 1999.

——— *Vive le matérialisme!* Lagrasse: Verdier, 2001.

——— with Christian Jambet. *L'Ange.* Paris: Grasset, 1976.

Larsson, Björn. *From Cape Wrath to Finisterre: Sailing the Celtic Fringe.* London: Haus, 2012.

Laruelle, François. *Biography of the Ordinary Man: Of Authorities and Minorities*, tr. J. Hock and A. Dubilet. Cambridge: Polity, 2018.

——— *Tétralogos.* Paris: Cerf, 2019.

Le Braz, Anatole. *La Bretagne à travers l'Histoire.* Paris: Les Équateurs, 2009.

Le Bris, Michel. *Un hiver en Bretagne.* Paris: Seuil, 1997.

Le Cloarec, Alain. *Aux origines des mouvements bretons.* Spézet: Coop Breizh, 2016.

Le Corre, Yvon. *L'Ivre de mer.* Tréguier, 2010.

Lecerf, Yannick. *La Bretagne préhistorique. Les peuplements, des origines à la conquête romaine.* Morlaix: Skol Vreizh, 2014.

——— 'Qu'on se le dise: les Bretons ne sont pas celtes'. *La Nouvelle République*, 25 November 2014.

——— *Bretons et Celtes. Quand le monde de l'archéologie s'interroge ou les incertitudes de la celtitude.* Le Coudray-Macouart: Feuillage, 2017.

Levinas, Emmanuel. *On Escape*, tr. B. Bergo. Stanford, CA: Stanford University Press, 2003.

Loyen, André. 'L'âme bretonne'. *Annales de Bretagne* 54:1 (1947).

Macé, Gérard. 'L'œuvre en miettes de Saint-Pol-Roux', in Saint-Pol-Roux, *Le Trésor de l'Homme.* Mortemart: Rougerie, 1991.

Madézo, Charles. *Portuaires.* Rennes: La Part Commune, 2008.

Melville, Herman. *Moby Dick.* Project Gutenberg eBook.

Michelet, Jules. *Histoire de France.* Paris: Lacroix, 1876.

Milner, Jean-Claude. 'Universality in Splinters', tr. P.-H. Monot. *Critical Inquiry* 46:1 (Autumn 2019).

BIBLIOGRAPHY

Moitessier, Bernard. *La Longue Route. Seul entre mers et ciels*. Paris: J'ai lu, 1994.

Novalis. *Notes for a Romantic Encyclopedia: Das Allgemeine Brouillon*, tr. ed. D.W. Wood. New York: SUNY Press, 2007.

Paulsson, Bettina Schulz. 'Radiocarbon Dates and Bayesian Modeling Support Maritime Diffusion Model for Megaliths in Europe'. *Proceedings of the National Academy of Sciences of the United States of America* 116:9 (26 February 2019), 3460–3465.

Pavese, Cesare. *This Business of Living: Diaries 1935–1950*. London and New York: Routledge, 2017.

Perros, Georges. *Œuvres*. Paris: Gallimard, 2017.

——— *Papiers collés I*. Paris: Gallimard, 2019.

——— *Poèmes bleus*. Paris: Gallimard, 2019.

Queffélec, Henri. *Tempête sur Douarnenez*. Paris: Mercure de France, 1951.

Quignard, Pascal. *Sur l'idée d'une communauté de solitaires*. Paris: Arléa, 2015.

Riboulet, Mathieu. *Le Corps des anges*. Paris: Gallimard, 2005.

Rousseau, Jean-Jacques. *Œuvres complètes*. Paris: Pléiade, 5 volumes, 1959–95.

——— *The Social Contract and Other Later Political Writings*, ed. V. Gourevitch. Cambridge: Cambridge University Press, 1997.

——— *Reveries of the Solitary Walker*. London: Penguin Classics, 2004.

Rousset, Emmanuelle. *L'Idéal chaviré*. Lagrasse: Verdier, 2000.

Saint-John Perse. *Seamarks*, tr. W. Fowley. New York: Harper, 1958.

——— *Collected Poems*. Princeton, NJ: Princeton University Press, 1983.

——— *Œuvres complètes*. Paris: Gallimard, 1982.

Saint-Pol-Roux [Paul-Pierre Roux]. *La Besace du solitaire*, ed. J. Goorma and A. Whyte. Mortemart: Rougerie, 2000.

——— *Le Trésor de l'Homme*, ed. G. Macé. Mortemart: Rougerie, 1991.

Salaün, Pierre. *Île de Sein*. Rennes: Éditions Ouest-France, 1997.

Sautter, Jean-Michel. *Mer des Hommes*. Louviers: L'Ancre de Marine, 2007.

Schoendoerffer, Pierre. *Le Crabe-tambour*. Paris: Grasset, 1976.

Starobinski, Jean. 'Démocrite parle. L'utopie mélancolique de Robert Burton'. *Le Débat* 29 (March 1984), 54–55.

Stiegler, Barbara. *« Il faut s'adapter ». Sur un nouvel impératif politique*. Paris: Gallimard, 2018.

Tabarly, Éric. *Mémoires du large*. Paris: Le Livre de Poche, 1998.

Valdinoci, Serge. *L'Europanalyse et les structures d'une autre vie. Le feu de la pensée sacrée*. Paris: L'Harmattan, 2001.

Veinstein, Alain. *Radio sauvage*. Paris: Seuil, 2010.

Weil, Simone. *Gravity and Grace*, tr. E. Crawford and M. von der Ruhr. London and New York: Routledge, 2002.

White, Kenneth. *En toute candeur*, tr. P. Leyris. Paris: Mercure de France, 1964.

——— *Le Lieu et la Parole. Entretiens 1987–1997*. Cléguer: Éditions du Scorff, 1997.

——— *Dialogue avec Deleuze. Politique, philosophie, géopoétique*. Paris: Isolato, 2007.

——— *Les Finisterres de l'esprit. Rimbaud, Segalen et moi-même*. Paris: Isolato, 2007.

Wittgenstein, Ludwig. *Culture and Value*, ed. G.H. von Wright with H. Nyman, tr. P. Winch. Chicago: University of Chicago Press, 1980.

Worms, Frédéric. 'L'ouverture, oui mais laquelle?'. *Libération*, 7 April, 2017.

Zizek, Slavoj. *Less Than Nothing: Hegel and the Shadow of Dialectical Materialism*. London and New York: Verso, 2012.

INDEX